Company's Coming®

Heart-Friendly

cooking low in fat & sodium

Heart-Friendly Cooking

Front and Back Covers

1. Pineapple Lemon Punch, page 31
2. Stuffed Peppers, page 123
3. Seafood Shells Vinaigrette, page 60
4. Grilled Vegetable Kabobs, page 112
5. Crisp Meringue Cream Pies, page 149
6. Chicken Spinach Strudel, page 85

Second printing February 2003

Canadian Cataloguing in Publication Data
Paré, Jean
    Heart-friendly cooking / Jean Paré.
(Lifestyle series)
Includes index.
At head of title: Company's Coming.
ISBN 1-895455-95-2
    1. Heart--Diseases--Diet therapy--Recipes. 2. Low-fat diet--Recipes.
3. Salt-free diet--Recipes. I. Title. II. Series: Paré, Jean. Lifestyle series.

RC684.D5P37 2003   641.5'6311   C2002-904539-8

Published simultaneously in
Canada and the United States of America
by Company's Coming
Publishing Limited
2311 - 96 Street
Edmonton, Alberta, Canada
T6N 1G3
Tel: 780 • 450-6223
Fax: 780 • 450-1857
www.companyscoming.com

Printed in Canada

We gratefully acknowledge the following suppliers for their generous support of our Test Kitchen and Photography Studio:

Broil King Barbecues
Corelle®
Lagostina

Our special thanks to the following businesses for providing various props for photography:

Anchor Hocking Canada
Bernardin Ltd.
Canhome Global
Casa Bugatti
Cherison Enterprises Inc.
Island Pottery Inc.
Linens 'N Things
Pfaltzgraff Canada
Stokes
The Bay
Wiltshire®

Company's Coming
COOKBOOKS

Visit us on-line

companyscoming.com

Who We Are | Browse Cookbooks | Cooking Tonight? | Home

everyday ingredients

feature recipes

feature recipes — Cooking tonight? Check out this month's *feature recipes*—absolutely FREE!

tips and tricks — Looking for some great kitchen helpers? *tips and tricks* is here to save the day!

reader circle — In search of answers to cooking or household questions? Do you have answers you'd like to share? Join the fun with *reader circle*, our on-line question and answer bulletin board. Our *reader circle chat room* connects you with cooks from around the world. Great for swapping recipes too!

cooking links — Other interesting and informative web-sites are just a click away with *cooking links.*

keyword search — Find cookbooks by title, description or food category using *keyword search*.

e-mail us — We want to hear from you—*e-mail us* lets you offer suggestions for upcoming titles, or share your favourite recipes.

Company's Coming
COOKBOOKS

Canada's
**most popular
cookbooks!**

Company's Coming
cookbooks

ORIGINAL SERIES

150 Delicious Squares	Starters
Casseroles	Stir-Fry
Muffins & More	Make-Ahead Meals
Salads	The Potato Book
Appetizers	Low-Fat Cooking
Desserts	Low-Fat Pasta
Soups & Sandwiches	Cook For Kids
Cookies	Stews, Chilies & Chowders
Pasta	Fondues
Barbecues	The Beef Book
Light Recipes	Asian Cooking
Preserves	The Cheese Book
Chicken, Etc.	The Rookie Cook
Kids Cooking	Rush-Hour Recipes
Breads	Sweet Cravings
Cooking For Two	Year-Round Grilling **NEW**
Breakfasts & Brunches	March 1, 2003
Slow Cooker Recipes	
One Dish Meals	

LIFESTYLE SERIES

Grilling
Diabetic Cooking
Heart-Friendly Cooking

GREATEST HITS

Italian
Mexican

SPECIAL OCCASION SERIES

Gifts from the Kitchen
Cooking for the Seasons
Home for the Holidays

Table of contents

The Company's Coming story

Jean Paré grew up understanding that the combination of family, friends and home cooking is the essence of a good life. From her mother she learned to appreciate good cooking, while her father praised even her earliest attempts. When she left home she took with her many acquired family recipes, a love of cooking and an intriguing desire to read recipe books like novels!

"never share a recipe you wouldn't use yourself"

In 1963, when her four children had all reached school age, Jean volunteered to cater the 50th anniversary of the Vermilion School of Agriculture, now Lakeland College. Working out of her home, Jean prepared a dinner for over 1000 people which launched a flourishing catering operation that continued for over eighteen years. During that time she was provided with countless opportunities to test new ideas with immediate feedback—resulting in empty plates and contented customers! Whether preparing cocktail sandwiches for a house party or serving a hot meal for 1500 people, Jean Paré earned a reputation for good food, courteous service and reasonable prices.

"Why don't you write a cookbook?" Time and again, as requests for her recipes mounted, Jean was asked that question. Jean's response was to team up with her son, Grant Lovig, in the fall of 1980 to form Company's Coming Publishing Limited. April 14, 1981, marked the debut of "150 DELICIOUS SQUARES", the first Company's Coming cookbook in what soon would become Canada's most popular cookbook series.

Jean Paré's operation has grown steadily from the early days of working out of a spare bedroom in her home. Full-time staff includes marketing personnel located in major cities across Canada. Home Office is based in Edmonton, Alberta in a modern building constructed specially for the company.

Today the company distributes throughout Canada and the United States in addition to numerous overseas markets, all under the guidance of Jean's daughter, Gail Lovig. Best-sellers many times over in English, Company's Coming cookbooks have also been published in French and Spanish. Familiar and trusted in home kitchens around the world, Company's Coming cookbooks are offered in a variety of formats, including the original softcover series.

Jean Paré's approach to cooking has always called for quick and easy recipes using everyday ingredients. Even when travelling, she is constantly on the lookout for new ideas to share with her readers. At home, she can usually be found researching and writing recipes, or working in the company's test kitchen. Jean continues to gain new supporters by adhering to what she  calls "the golden rule of cooking": never share a recipe you wouldn't use yourself. It's an approach that works— *millions of times over!*

foreword

Healthy living is a concern for a growing number of people today. We exercise more, balance work with leisure, and are more educated about what we eat. It used to be widely believed that if something tasted good, it wasn't good for you. Likewise, if something tasted bad, then likely it was good for you! But with the research available today and an increasingly adventurous approach to food, this accepted "truth" has been largely debunked.

We have seen nutrition fads come and go but one rule has remained steadfast—a diet high in fat and salt increases the risk of heart disease, hypertension, stroke, diabetes, obesity, and some cancers. *Heart-Friendly Cooking* is for people who insist on great tasting meals, whether they are on calorie, salt and fat-reduced diets or are just concerned about what they eat. Each recipe has been tested and analyzed to ensure that it is nutritionally sound, heart friendly, and delicious.

We have included many tips to change cooking and eating habits that will decrease the amount of fat you use and encourage more fruits and vegetables in your diet. We have also experimented with herbs and spices that will complement and enhance the natural flavour of ingredients without reaching for the salt. For example, coriander and cilantro (different parts of the same plant) and cumin, all of the parsley family, have become increasingly popular in recent years. The more familiar you become with these new and refreshing flavours, the more you will enjoy them and the less you will miss the salt. And you can always reduce or omit a seasoning that is not your favourite. The resulting taste will differ from the original—but still be good! For those who are not on salt-reduced diets, add a very light sprinkle of salt at the table rather than while cooking. You will find that you use much less this way because the salt hits your taste buds right away!

So approach these recipes with a new attitude! Be adventurous and let *Heart-Friendly Cooking* help you expand your cupboard "basics" to give you more options when preparing meals. Enjoy introducing your family and friends to exciting new dishes that are not only delicious but also good to your heart.

Jean Paré

Nutrition Information

Each recipe has been analyzed using the most up-to-date version of the Canadian Nutrient File from Health Canada, which is based on the United States Department of Agriculture (USDA) Nutrient Data Base. If more than one ingredient is listed (such as "hard margarine or butter"), the first ingredient is used in the analysis. Where an ingredient reads "sprinkle," "optional," or "for garnish," it is not included as part of the nutrition information.

Heather Schnurr
Registered Dietitian

About Heart Disease

Heart disease is the leading cause of death in North America and a major cause of illnesses such as stroke, poor circulation and angina, a symptom of coronary artery disease. Having a healthy heart is vital for living a longer and fuller life. A poorly functioning heart leaves you feeling tired and short of breath which limits the quality of your life. The well-known risk factors leading to heart disease are: high blood cholesterol, high blood pressure, being overweight, lack of exercise, cigarette smoking, diabetes, aging and family history of heart disease. Many of these factors are related to lifestyle choices.

Heart disease is more likely to develop if you have high levels of cholesterol in your blood, especially low-density lipoproteins (LDL or "bad" cholesterol). Cholesterol is a waxy substance that is needed by all our cells. Our liver packages cholesterol in LDL particles and feeds it into our blood. Cholesterol is removed from our blood when packaged in high-density lipoproteins (HDL or "good" cholesterol). While in the blood, these LDL-Cholesterol packages damage and then collect on the walls of your arteries. Over time, "fatty plaques" build up, narrowing arteries and reducing the flow of oxygen-rich blood. When your arteries are about 75% blocked, you can get a warning—chest pains (angina). A heart attack occurs when blood forms a clot totally blocking the flow of blood to your heart. A stroke occurs when the blood flow is blocked in an artery flowing to the brain.

The next time you have your blood cholesterol checked, look at the levels of these two types of cholesterol. The goal is to have high levels of HDL-Cholesterol and low levels of LDL-Cholesterol. Exercise can increase your HDL while a lower-fat diet can decrease your LDL.

High blood pressure is another risk factor which also can be controlled by diet and maintaining a healthy body weight. A diet low in salt and high in fruits, vegetables and low-fat dairy products can lower blood pressure. Regular exercise and a prudent diet that is low in fat are necessary to maintain a healthy body weight and a healthy heart.

Just a sprinkling... According to tests done with staff in the Company's Coming Test Kitchen, just a sprinkling of salt is less than 1/16 tsp. (0.5 mL). 1 tsp. (5 mL) salt = 2325 mg sodium. If your recipe calls for 2 tsp. (10 mL) salt, you've just added 4650 mg sodium to the recipe. If the recipe serves 4, each person will be consuming 1162 mg sodium. If you don't add salt to the recipe and just sprinkle it on at the table, each person will only add about 290 mg sodium—a far better choice!

Heart-Friendly Habits

Blood cholesterol is influenced by genetics and diet. For many people, a diet high in fat, especially saturated and trans fatty acids, raises total blood cholesterol and in particular, LDL-Cholesterol. When high cholesterol is a result of genetics, medication as well as diet is necessary to achieve healthy levels.

Health professionals recommend the following guidelines for those wishing to maintain a heart-healthy diet:

1 Your daily diet should consist of no more than 30% of total calories from all dietary fats. In other words, consume, on average, no more than 65 grams total fat (20 grams of saturated and trans fatty acids) daily for women and 90 grams total fat (40 grams of saturated and trans fatty acids) daily for men. Saturated fats are found in meat products, butter, lard, full-fat dairy products, palm oil and coconut oil. Trans fatty acids are fats formed during the hardening process of unsaturated oils. Trans fatty acids and palm and coconut oils are found in many margarines, shortening, store-bought baked goods, snack foods, cake mixes and frozen dinners.

Monounsaturated fats can help lower LDL-Cholesterol. They are found in olive, canola and peanut oils as well as some soft margarines, peanuts and almonds. Polyunsaturated fats can help lower LDL-Cholesterol but they also lower HDL-Cholesterol. They are found in corn, sunflower, safflower, soybean and sesame oils as well as some soft margarines and some nuts.

Omega 3 fats work in a variety of ways to reduce the risk of stroke and heart disease. They are found in cold water fish such as salmon, lake trout, herring, sardines and mackerel.

Limit cholesterol to 300 mg daily (200 mg if you have high cholesterol). Foods high in cholesterol include egg yolks, organ meats such as liver and full-fat dairy products (whole milk, cream, cheeses and butter).

2 Use less salt (no more than 3000 mg of sodium per day for the average person). A high-salt diet can contribute to high blood pressure. Sodium is found in table salt, cured meats such as bacon and ham, condiments, olives, pickles, tomato juice and many commercially prepared foods.

3 Aim for six or more servings per day of fruits and vegetables. Choose whole grain foods such as whole wheat and whole grain breads, brown rice and whole wheat pastas. These foods provide nutrients which help maintain a healthy heart. Soluble fibre reduces blood cholesterol levels. It is found in oat products, legumes (dried beans, peas and lentils) and pectin-rich fruits such as apples, citrus fruits and strawberries.

Use Canada's Food Guide to Healthy Eating to help you eat a balanced diet. This pamphlet is available from your local health professional, Health Canada or the Health Canada web site. Choose a variety of foods from within each food group to obtain all the vitamins and minerals you need daily. Limit the number of "other foods" such as soft drinks, candy and snack foods. These are low in nutrients and high in fat, sugar, salt and/or energy. Balance the number of food choices with your energy needs to help maintain a healthy weight.

Heather Schnurr, R.D.
With thanks to Pamela Monkhouse, R.D.

The Recipes in this Cookbook

We have provided recipes for making your own stocks and some condiments in order to reduce the fat and sodium content that these ingredients add to daily nutrition. Throughout the cookbook, these basic recipes have been used in other recipes, in some cases two or three may be used in one recipe. If you are on a restricted diet, these recipes will be worth the added time to make and have on hand. If you are not, you certainly may choose to use the commercially prepared versions of these ingredients. Just be mindful that the nutrition information will change, increasing the fat and sodium levels. Although the recipes in this cookbook use low-fat or non-fat products as well as lower sodium products, they will be successful with the regular version of these ingredients.

Fats: The majority of recipes in this book provide a serving size that contains less than 25% of calories from fat (less than 5 grams of total fat and 2 grams of saturated fats along with less than 25 mg of cholesterol). Canola or olive oil was used instead of hard margarine or butter to reduce the amount of saturated fats. All added fats were used in limited amounts. Where possible, we used non-stick cookware or cooking spray.

Egg Substitutes: Egg substitutes were used when more than two eggs were needed or when the recipe was considered an "egg" dish or was already higher in saturated fats. You may also choose to use "designer eggs" which contain less cholesterol and saturated fats.

Meats: Meats used were lean cuts such as boneless, skinless chicken or turkey breasts, pork tenderloin or beef sirloin trimmed of fat prior to cooking. Fish and seafood were used to provide a good source of protein.

Dairy Products: These recipes were tested with 1% milk, skim evaporated milk, skim milk buttermilk, plain and flavoured low-fat (1%) yogurt, light sharp Cheddar cheese and part-skim mozzarella cheese—all to lower the fat content without compromising the taste.

Sodium: We have provided low-salt recipes for traditionally high-salt staples such as stewed tomatoes, ketchup and stocks. By using these "basics," along with fresh herbs and minimal added salt, we have produced recipes suitable for those on a salt-restricted diet. In fact, many of these recipes are so low in sodium, you may even be able to add a sprinkle of salt at the table, depending on the dietary guidelines provided by your health professional.

Fresh Herbs: We have used an abundance of fresh herbs in these recipes to add loads of flavour without relying on salt. Keep fresh herbs wrapped in a slightly damp paper towel inside a tightly closed plastic bag. Blow into the bag before sealing. The carbon dioxide will help to keep them fresh. Store in the refrigerator.

Cooking Methods: Recommended methods include baking, grilling, steaming, poaching and stir-frying to reduce the amount of fat needed to cook an item.

Chicken Stock

A classic chicken stock recipe that can be used in any number of soups, casseroles and stews. This homemade version is very low in sodium.

Chicken necks, backs and wings	5 – 6 lbs.	2.3 – 2.7 kg
Dry white (or alcohol-free) wine	1 cup	250 mL
Water	12 cups	3 L
Large carrots, with peel, chopped	4	4
Celery ribs, chopped	3	3
Large leeks (white and tender parts only), halved	2	2
Whole black peppercorns	12	12
Bunch of fresh parsley, stalks only (see Note)	1	1
Bay leaves	2	2

Combine all 9 ingredients in large stock pot. Bring to a boil on medium-high. Reduce heat to low. Simmer, uncovered, without stirring, for 3 hours, occasionally skimming any foam and fat from surface. Strain through fine sieve into large bowl. Discard solids. Cool. Cover. Chill overnight. Discard layer of fat from stock. Freeze in 1 cup (250 mL) portions in airtight containers for up to 6 months. Makes about 8 cups (2 L).

1 cup (250 mL): 35 Calories; 1.7 g Total Fat (0.5 g Mono, 0.3 g Poly, 0.5 g Sat); 2 mg Cholesterol; 1 g Carbohydrate; 0 g Fibre; 4 g Protein; 27 mg Sodium

Note: Use only the stalks of parsley to keep stock clear and full of flavour. The leaves have the highest concentration of chlorophyll and will leach colour into the stock. The stalks have more intense flavour than the leaves.

Used as an ingredient in the following recipes:

Roasted Pepper Sushi, page 22
Split Pea Dip And Pitas, page 26
Mushroom And Herb Pie, page 49
Lebanese Fattoush Salad, page 62
Couscous And Bean Salad, page 63
Mulligatawny Soup, page 67
Full O' Beans Soup, page 68
Chicken Tomato Soup, page 69
Creamy Yam Soup, page 70
Cheesy Broccoli Soup, page 73
Cream Of Asparagus Soup, page 75
Philippines Stew, page 81

Cacciatore Casserole, page 82
Chicken Meatballs, page 83
Chicken Stew, page 87
Seafood Stew, page 93
Seafood Pasta Salad, page 100
Halibut Stir-Fry, page 101
Chewy Wheat Pilaf, page 106
Vegetable Chickpea Curry, page 116
Minted Peas And Beans, page 128
Creamy Polenta, page 129
Pesto, page 132

Beef Stock

Delicious beef stock that is aromatic and rich in colour. This homemade stock is an excellent base for soups and chilies and is very low in sodium.

Beef bones and trimmings	9 lbs.	4 kg
Large carrots, with peel, chopped	4	4
Large onions, with peel, quartered	3	3
Celery ribs, chopped	3	3
Water	24 cups	6 L
Bunch of fresh parsley, stalks only (see Note)	1	1
Sprigs of fresh thyme	6	6
Whole black peppercorns	16	16
Bay leaves	2	2

Combine first 4 ingredients on 2 baking sheets. Bake in 375°F (190°C) oven for about 1 1/2 hours, stirring occasionally, until browned. Transfer to large stock pot.

Add remaining 5 ingredients. Bring to a boil on medium-high. Reduce heat to medium-low. Simmer, uncovered, without stirring, for 6 hours, occasionally skimming any foam and fat from surface. Strain through fine sieve into large bowl. Discard solids. Cool. Cover. Chill overnight. Discard layer of fat from stock. Freeze in 1 cup (250 mL) portions in airtight containers for up to 6 months. Makes about 12 cups (3 L).

1 cup (250 mL): 39 Calories; 1.5 g Total Fat (0.3 g Mono, 0.2 g Poly, 0.2 g Sat); 1 mg Cholesterol; 2 g Carbohydrate; trace Fibre; 4 g Protein; 24 mg Sodium

Note: Use only the stalks of parsley to keep stock clear and full of flavour. The leaves have the highest concentration of chlorophyll and will leach colour into the stock. The stalks have more intense flavour than the leaves.

Used as an ingredient in the following recipes:

Spinach And Meatball Soup, page 74
Beef And Lentil Chili, page 76

Vegetable Stock

A versatile homemade vegetable stock that is ideal for meatless recipes. Makes a savoury base for a stir-fry, pesto and more. Very low in sodium.

Dry white (or alcohol-free) wine	**2 cups**	**500 mL**
Water	**8 cups**	**2 L**
Celery ribs, chopped	**3**	**3**
Large carrots, peeled and chopped	**4**	**4**
Large onions, with peel, chopped	**2**	**2**
Bay leaves	**2**	**2**
Whole black peppercorns	**10**	**10**

Combine all 7 ingredients in large pot or Dutch oven. Bring to a boil on medium-high. Reduce heat to medium-low. Simmer, uncovered, without stirring, for 30 minutes, occasionally skimming any foam from surface. Strain through fine sieve into large bowl. Discard solids. Cool. Freeze in 1 cup (250 mL) portions in airtight containers for up to 6 months. Makes about 8 cups (2 L).

1 cup (250 mL): 16 Calories; 0.5 g Total Fat (0.1 g Mono, 0.1 g Poly, trace Sat); 0 mg Cholesterol; 2 g Carbohydrate; trace Fibre; 1 g Protein; 16 mg Sodium

Used as an ingredient in the following recipes:

Mushroom And Herb Pie, page 49

Lettuce Parcels, page 57

Mulligatawny Soup, page 67

Tofu Chili Stir-Fry, page 105

Barley Risotto, page 119

Stuffed Peppers, page 123

Creamy Polenta, page 129

Pesto, page 132

Black Beans

Hearty, filling black beans are a great high fibre addition to salsa or veggie burgers. Use mashed in place of meat in tacos and burritos.

Dried black beans (about 2 1/4 cups, 550 mL)	**1 lb.**	**454 g**
Water, to cover		
Water	**14 cups**	**3.5 L**
Sprigs of fresh thyme (or 1 tsp., 5 mL, dried)	**4**	**4**
Garlic cloves, peeled (or 1 tsp., 5 mL, powder)	**4**	**4**
Strip of lemon peel (about 3 inch, 7.5 cm, length)	**1**	**1**

(continued on next page)

Soak black beans in first amount of water in large bowl overnight. Drain. Put into large pot or Dutch oven.

Add remaining 4 ingredients. Bring to a boil on medium-high. Reduce heat to medium-low. Cover. Simmer for about 55 minutes until beans are softened but not mushy. Drain. Remove and discard thyme, garlic and lemon peel. Rinse beans under cold water. Drain well. Freeze in 1 cup (250 mL) portions in airtight containers or resealable freezer bags. Makes about 6 cups (1.5 L).

1 cup (250 mL): 238 Calories; 1 g Total Fat (0 g Mono, 0.4 g Poly, 0.3 g Sat); 0 mg Cholesterol; 43 g Carbohydrate; 16 g Fibre; 16 g Protein; 2 mg Sodium

Used as an ingredient in the following recipe:

Beef And Eggplant Burgers, page 78

Chickpeas

Chickpeas are frequently added to soups, salads and stews and add a lot of fibre too. Process in a food processor until smooth to make dips, such as hummus, or to use as a burger base.

Dried chickpeas (garbanzo beans), about 2 1/4 cups (550 mL)	**1 lb.**	**454 g**
Water, to cover		
Water	**14 cups**	**3.5 L**

Soak chickpeas in first amount of water in large bowl overnight. Drain. Put into large pot or Dutch oven.

Add second amount of water. Bring to a boil on medium-high. Reduce heat to medium-low. Cover. Simmer for about 45 minutes until chickpeas are softened but not mushy. Drain. Rinse under cold water. Drain well. Freeze in 1 cup (250 mL) portions in airtight containers or resealable freezer bags. Makes about 6 cups (1.5 L).

1 cup (250 mL): 263 Calories; 4.2 g Total Fat (0.9 g Mono, 1.9 g Poly, 0.4 g Sat); 0 mg Cholesterol; 44 g Carbohydrate; 12 g Fibre; 14 g Protein; 11 mg Sodium

Used as an ingredient in the following recipes:

Couscous And Bean Salad, page 63
Chicken Tomato Soup, page 69
Philippines Stew, page 81

Spiced Lamb Stew, page 103
Vegetable Chickpea Curry, page 116
Pesto, page 132

Green Lentils

A healthy addition to chilies and casseroles.

Dried green lentils (about 2 1/3 cups, 575 mL)	**1 lb.**	**454 g**
Water	**8 cups**	**2 L**
Small onion	**1/2**	**1/2**
Garlic clove (or 1/4 tsp., 1 mL, powder)	**1**	**1**
Sprig of fresh thyme	**1**	**1**
Bay leaf	**1**	**1**

Combine all 6 ingredients in large heavy pot or Dutch oven. Bring to a boil on medium-high. Reduce heat to medium-low. Simmer, uncovered, for about 20 minutes until lentils are softened but not mushy. Drain. Remove and discard onion, garlic clove, thyme sprig and bay leaf. Rinse lentils under cold water. Drain well. Freeze in 1 cup (250 mL) portions in airtight containers or resealable freezer bags. Makes about 7 cups (1.75 L).

1 cup (250 mL): 228 Calories; trace Total Fat (0 g Mono, trace Poly, trace Sat); 0 mg Cholesterol; 41 g Carbohydrate; 11 g Fibre; 17 g Protein; 23 mg Sodium

Used as an ingredient in the following recipes:

Beef And Lentil Chili, page 76 Curry Tomato Lentils, page 120
Oriental Lentil Packets, page 110

1. Split Pea Dip And Pitas, page 26
2. Bruschetta, page 29, on Country Seed Bread, page 39
3. Prawn And Pepper Skewers, page 27

Navy Beans

Navy beans are low in fat, high in fibre, tasty and wonderfully versatile.

Dried navy beans (about 2 1/4 cups, 550 mL) **Water, to cover**	**1 lb.**	**454 g**
Water	**8 cups**	**2 L**

Soak beans in first amount of water in large bowl overnight. Drain. Put into large pot or Dutch oven.

Add second amount of water. Bring to a boil on medium-high. Reduce heat to medium-low. Cover. Simmer for 45 to 50 minutes until beans are softened but not mushy. Drain. Rinse under cold water. Drain well. Freeze in 1 cup (250 mL) portions in airtight containers or resealable freezer bags. Makes about 6 cups (1.5 L).

1 cup (250 mL): 246 Calories; 1 g Total Fat (0.1 g Mono, 0.4 g Poly, 0.3 g Sat); 0 mg Cholesterol; 46 g Carbohydrate; 11 g Fibre; 15 g Protein; 2 mg Sodium

Used as an ingredient in the following recipes:

Spinach Yam Salad, page 58
Seafood Stew, page 93

Beans With Roasted Squash, page 122
Minted Peas And Beans, page 128

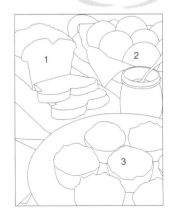

1. Whole Grain Bread, page 40
2. Whole Wheat Buns, page 42
3. Pineapple Bran Muffins, page 34

Stewed Tomatoes

These home-stewed tomatoes have a tangy flavour with a subtle hint of celery, onion and sweet basil. Use to make a delicious spaghetti sauce or as a base in any recipe that calls for stewed tomatoes. Quadruple the recipe to use up your tomato crop and cook in a 6 quart (6 L) slow cooker.

Whole ripe tomatoes (about 4 medium)	**2 lbs.**	**900 g**
Boiling water	**8 cups**	**2 L**
Finely chopped celery	**1/2 cup**	**125 mL**
Finely chopped onion	**1/2 cup**	**125 mL**
Finely chopped green pepper	**2 tbsp.**	**30 mL**
Dried sweet basil	**1/2 tsp.**	**2 mL**
Bay leaf	**1**	**1**
Granulated sugar	**1 tsp.**	**5 mL**
Parsley flakes	**1/2 tsp.**	**2 mL**
Salt	**1/4 tsp.**	**1 mL**
Pepper, just a pinch		

Drop tomatoes into boiling water in large pot or Dutch oven. Cook for about 2 minutes until skins begin to split. Remove and discard skins. Dice tomatoes, reserving any juice. Put tomato and juice into 3 1/2 quart (3.5 L) slow cooker.

Add remaining 9 ingredients. Stir. Cover. Cook on Low for 8 to 9 hours or on High for 4 to 4 1/2 hours until tomato is very soft. Remove and discard bay leaf. Freeze in 1 cup (250 mL) portions in airtight containers or resealable freezer bags. Makes about 2 2/3 cups (650 mL).

1 cup (250 mL): 96 Calories; 1.3 g Total Fat (0.2 g Mono, 0.5 g Poly, 0.2 g Sat); 0 mg Cholesterol; 21 g Carbohydrate; 4 g Fibre; 4 g Protein; 233 mg Sodium

Used as an ingredient in the following recipes:

Vegetable Pouches

These delicious little packets are flavoured with spicy ginger and dramatic mint. Save time by using the food processor to finely chop vegetables. These are irresistible when dipped in the sauce.

VEGETABLE FILLING		
Finely chopped spinach, packed	1 cup	250 mL
Finely chopped yam	1/2 cup	125 mL
Finely chopped red pepper	1/2 cup	125 mL
Finely chopped green onion	1/4 cup	60 mL
Finely grated gingerroot (or 1/8 tsp., 0.5 mL, ground ginger)	1/2 tsp.	2 mL
Garlic cloves, minced (or 1/2 tsp., 2 mL, powder)	2	2
Chopped fresh mint leaves (or 3/4 – 2 1/4 tsp., 4 – 11 mL, dried)	1 – 3 tbsp.	15 – 50 mL
Round dumpling wrappers	20	20
SAUCE		
Water	2 tbsp.	30 mL
Lime juice	1 tbsp.	15 mL
Sweet (or regular) chili sauce	1 tbsp.	15 mL
Low-sodium soy sauce	2 tsp.	10 mL

Vegetable Filling: Combine first 6 ingredients in non-stick wok or frying pan. Stir-fry on medium-high for 5 to 7 minutes until vegetables are tender-crisp.

Add mint. Stir. Makes 7/8 cup (200 mL) filling.

Brush wrappers lightly with water. Place 2 tsp. (10 mL) filling on centre of each wrapper. Bring wrapper edge together in centre to form pouch. Pinch and twist to seal about 1/3 inch (1 cm) from top. Line bottom of large bamboo steamer or regular steamer basket with parchment paper. Spray with cooking spray. Arrange pouches in single layer in steamer. Place bamboo steamer in wok on rack, or place steamer basket in pan, over simmering water. Cover. Steam on medium-low for about 20 minutes until wrappers are translucent and tender.

Sauce: Combine all 4 ingredients in small bowl. Makes 1/3 cup (75 mL) sauce. Serve with vegetable pouches. Makes 20 vegetable pouches.

1 vegetable pouch with 1 tsp. (5 mL) sauce: 28 Calories; 0.2 g Total Fat (trace Mono, 0.1 g Poly, 0.1 g Sat); 0 mg Cholesterol; 6 g Carbohydrate; trace Fibre; 1 g Protein; 30 mg Sodium

Roasted Pepper Sushi

These attractive, colourful sushi pinwheels will delight the eyes and taste buds of your guests.
These will become a favourite!

Large peppers (use combination of red, orange and yellow)	**4**	**4**
Chicken Stock, page 12	**1 cup**	**250 mL**
Rice vinegar	**1 tbsp.**	**15 mL**
Granulated sugar	**2 tsp.**	**10 mL**
Short grain white rice, uncooked	**2/3 cup**	**150 mL**
Sake (rice wine) or dry sherry	**1 tbsp.**	**15 mL**
Sesame oil (optional)	**1 tsp.**	**5 mL**
Chopped fresh parsley (or 3/4 tsp., 4 mL, flakes)	**1 tbsp.**	**15 mL**
Capers, chopped (optional)	**2 tsp.**	**10 mL**
Lemon pepper	**1/4 tsp.**	**1 mL**
Sesame seeds, toasted (see Tip, page 29)	**1 tsp.**	**5 mL**
Nori (roasted seaweed) sheets	**4**	**4**

Broil peppers 4 inches (10 cm) from heat or cook on greased electric grill, turning occasionally, until skins are completely blistered and blackened. Immediately place peppers in large bowl. Cover tightly with plastic wrap. Let sweat for about 20 minutes until cool enough to handle. Working over same bowl, cut peppers in half lengthwise. Scrape skin, stems and seeds into bowl. Strain, reserving 1/3 cup (75 mL) liquid. Add water to reserved liquid if necessary. Discard solids. Trim pepper halves to straighten edges and flatten.

Place reserved liquid in medium saucepan. Add stock, rice vinegar and sugar. Stir. Bring to a boil.

Add rice. Stir. Reduce heat to low. Cover. Simmer for about 15 minutes until liquid is absorbed and rice is tender. Remove from heat.

Add next 6 ingredients. Stir. Cool to room temperature. Makes 1 2/3 cups (400 mL) rice mixture.

1) Place 1 nori sheet on bamboo mat or heavy cloth napkin, smooth side down, to assist in rolling. Place 2 pepper halves, end to end, about 1 inch (2.5 cm) from edge of nori sheet. 2) Spread about 6 tbsp. (100 mL) rice mixture on peppers, using wet hands or spatula, in even layer. Brush uncovered top portion of nori sheet with water. 3) Roll up from bottom edge to top, using bamboo mat and pressing lightly to enclose peppers and rice tightly in nori. Repeat with remaining nori, pepper halves and rice. Trim up to 1 inch (2.5 cm) from ends of rolls (depending on size of peppers and how close to the edge of the nori they come) with wet sharp knife, to even out peppers and nori. Cut remainder into 3/4 inch (2 cm) slices. Makes 4 rolls, each cutting into about 8 slices, for a total of about 32 slices.

(continued on next page)

1 slice: 18 Calories; 0.2 g Total Fat (trace Mono, 0.1 g Poly, trace Sat); trace Cholesterol; 4 g Carbohydrate; trace Fibre; 1 g Protein; 5 mg Sodium

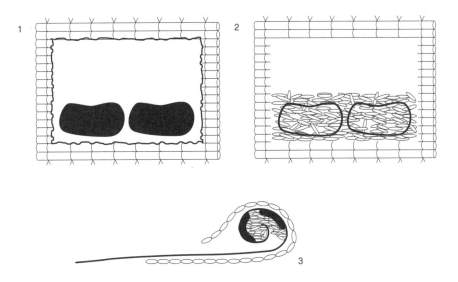

Spicy Salmon Fritters

This simple and healthy treat is crispy golden on the outside, warm and soft on the inside. Serve with a dollop of sour cream and garnish with fresh parsley. Perfect as an appetizer, snack or light meal.

Whole wheat flour	**1/4 cup**	**60 mL**
All-purpose flour	**1/4 cup**	**60 mL**
Baking powder	**1 tsp.**	**5 mL**
Cans of red salmon (7 1/2 oz., 213 g, each), drained, skin and round bones removed	**2**	**2**
Can of salt-reduced kernel corn, drained	**12 oz.**	**341 mL**
Large egg, fork-beaten	**1**	**1**
Milk	**3 tbsp.**	**50 mL**
Chopped fresh parsley (or cilantro)	**1 – 3 tbsp.**	**15 – 50 mL**
Sliced pickled jalapeño pepper	**1 tbsp.**	**15 mL**

Combine both flours and baking powder in large bowl.

Add remaining 6 ingredients. Mix well. Form into 9 patties, using about 1/3 cup (75 mL) for each. Spray large non-stick frying pan with cooking spray. Cook fritters, in 2 batches, on medium-high for 2 to 3 minutes per side until golden. Makes 9 fritters.

1 fritter: 117 Calories; 3.7 g Total Fat (1.5 g Mono, 0.9 g Poly, 0.9 g Sat); 41 mg Cholesterol; 11 g Carbohydrate; 1 g Fibre; 10 g Protein; 304 mg Sodium

Stuffed Vine Leaves

You can imagine you are in Greece as you enjoy the taste of grapevine leaves stuffed with spiced beef, currants, tomatoes and fresh mint. Serve with a zesty wedge of lemon.

Finely chopped onion	1/2 cup	125 mL
Garlic cloves, minced (or 1/2 tsp., 2 mL, powder)	2	2
Olive (or canola) oil	1 tsp.	5 mL
Ground cumin	1/4 – 1 tsp.	1 – 5 mL
Ground coriander	1/4 – 1 tsp.	1 – 5 mL
Ground cinnamon	1/8 – 1/2 tsp.	0.5 – 2 mL
Lean ground beef	6 oz.	170 g
Brown converted rice, uncooked	3 tbsp.	50 mL
Currants	2 tbsp.	30 mL
Water	2 tbsp.	30 mL
Chopped fresh mint leaves (or 3/4 – 2 1/4 tsp., 4 – 11 mL, dried)	1 – 3 tbsp.	15 – 50 mL
Grapevine leaves	18	18
Cold water, to cover		
Stewed Tomatoes, with juice, page 20	1 1/2 cups	375 mL
Lemon juice	3 tbsp.	50 mL
Granulated sugar	1 tsp.	5 mL

Sauté onion and garlic in olive oil in large non-stick frying pan for about 5 minutes until soft.

Add cumin, coriander and cinnamon. Heat and stir for about 1 minute until fragrant. Put into medium bowl.

Add next 5 ingredients. Mix well.

Put grapevine leaves into large bowl. Cover with cold water. Let stand for 5 minutes. Drain. Rinse under cold water. Drain well. Place grapevine leaves, vein-side up, on work surface. Spoon 1 tbsp. (15 mL) filling down centre of each leaf. Fold in both sides of leaves over filling. Roll up from bottom to enclose filling. Set fairly flat plate to fit in bottom of large saucepan. Arrange rolls in single layer, seam-side down, on plate.

(continued on next page)

Process tomatoes with juice, lemon juice and sugar in food processor until smooth. Makes about 1 2/3 cups (400 mL) sauce. Pour over rolls. Invert another plate over tomato mixture to weight rolls down. Bring tomato mixture to a boil. Reduce heat to low. Cover. Simmer for about 1 hour until leaves are tender. Makes 18 stuffed leaves.

1 stuffed leaf: 50 Calories; 2.1 g Total Fat (0.9 g Mono, 0.2 g Poly, 0.7 g Sat); 7 mg Cholesterol; 6 g Carbohydrate; 1 g Fibre; 3 g Protein; 140 mg Sodium

Stuffed Mushrooms

Who can resist the taste of plump, juicy mushrooms stuffed with shrimp, garlic, dill and Parmesan cheese? These are easy to prepare, so make extra to replenish the platter.

Finely chopped green onion	**3 tbsp.**	**50 mL**
Garlic cloves, minced (or 1/2 tsp., 2 mL, powder)	**2**	**2**
Olive (or canola) oil	**2 tsp.**	**10 mL**
Raw medium shrimp, peeled, deveined and finely chopped	**12 oz.**	**340 g**
Chopped fresh dill (or 3/4 tsp., 4 mL, dill weed)	**1 tbsp.**	**15 mL**
Pepper	**1/4 tsp.**	**1 mL**
Fresh whole wheat bread crumbs	**2 tbsp.**	**30 mL**
Finely grated fresh Parmesan cheese	**2 tbsp.**	**30 mL**
Brown (cremini), or white, mushrooms, about 2 inches (5 cm) in diameter, stems removed	**20**	**20**

Sauté green onion and garlic in olive oil in frying pan for about 5 minutes until soft.

Add shrimp, dill and pepper. Heat and stir for about 2 minutes until shrimp is pink. Remove from heat.

Add bread crumbs and Parmesan cheese. Mix well.

Stuff mushroom caps with shrimp mixture. Arrange on ungreased baking sheet. Bake in 475°F (240°C) oven for 5 to 8 minutes until mushrooms are just cooked and shrimp mixture is golden brown. Makes 20 stuffed mushrooms.

1 stuffed mushroom: 26 Calories; 0.8 g Total Fat (0.4 g Mono, 0.1 g Poly, 0.2 g Sat); 21 mg Cholesterol; 2 g Carbohydrate; trace Fibre; 3 g Protein; 43 mg Sodium

Split Pea Dip And Pitas

A scrumptious dip to enjoy with Baked Pita Dippers, below, Country Seed Bread, page 39, veggies or corn chips. Add more chili powder to suit your taste.

SPLIT PEA DIP

Water	4 cups	1 L
Yellow split peas, rinsed and drained	1 cup	250 mL
Chopped onion	3/4 cup	175 mL
Garlic clove, minced (or 1/4 tsp., 1 mL, powder)	1	1
Strip of lemon peel (about 3 inch, 7.5 cm, length)	1	1
Sprig of fresh rosemary (about 3 inch, 7.5 cm, length)	1	1
Chopped potato	1 1/2 cups	375 mL
Chicken Stock, page 12	1 1/2 cups	375 mL
Finely chopped green onion	1/3 cup	75 mL
Olive (or canola) oil	1 tbsp.	15 mL
Lemon juice	1 tbsp.	15 mL
Ground cumin	1/4 – 1/2 tsp.	1 – 2 mL
Ground coriander	1/4 – 1/2 tsp.	1 – 2 mL
Chili powder	1/2 tsp.	2 mL

BAKED PITA DIPPERS

Whole wheat pita breads (about 6 inches, 15 cm)	8	8
Finely grated fresh Parmesan cheese	2 tbsp.	30 mL
Chili powder	1/4 tsp.	1 mL

Split Pea Dip: Combine first 6 ingredients in large saucepan. Bring to a boil. Reduce heat to medium-low. Simmer, uncovered, for about 1 hour, stirring occasionally, until split peas are tender. Drain, reserving 1/2 cup (125 mL) liquid. Remove and discard lemon peel and rosemary sprig. Put split pea mixture into food processor. Add reserved liquid. Process until smooth.

Cook potato in stock in separate large saucepan for about 15 minutes until tender. Drain. Mash until no lumps remain.

Add split pea mixture and next 6 ingredients. Stir until well combined. Makes about 4 cups (1 L) dip.

(continued on next page)

Baked Pita Dippers: Place pitas on ungreased baking sheets. Spray with cooking spray. Sprinkle with Parmesan cheese and chili powder. Bake in 350°F (175°C) oven for 10 to 12 minutes until crisp. Break into 2 inch (5 cm) pieces. Serve with dip.

1/4 cup (60 mL) dip with 5 dippers: 157 Calories; 2.4 g Total Fat (1 g Mono, 0.6 g Poly, 0.5 g Sat); 1 mg Cholesterol; 29 g Carbohydrate; 6 g Fibre; 7 g Protein; 267 mg Sodium

Pictured on page 17.

Prawn And Pepper Skewers

These delicious skewers look as good as they taste. The marinade mixture is fresh, spicy, sweet and savoury, all in one. These are surprisingly easy and fun to prepare.

Pepitas (see Note), toasted (see Tip, page 29)	1/2 cup	125 mL
Fresh cilantro (or parsley) leaves, packed	1 – 4 tbsp.	15 – 60 mL
Lemon juice	2 tbsp.	30 mL
Garlic clove	1	1
Chili paste (sambal oelek)	1 – 2 tsp.	5 – 10 mL
Granulated sugar	1 tsp.	5 mL
Ground cumin (optional)	1/4 – 1 tsp.	1 – 5 mL
Raw large shrimp, peeled and deveined, leaving tails intact	24	24
Small red pepper, cut into 3/4 inch (2 cm) pieces	1	1
Small yellow pepper, cut into 3/4 inch (2 cm) pieces	1	1
Bamboo skewers, 8 inch (20 cm) length, soaked in water for 10 minutes	8	8

Put first 7 ingredients into food processor. Process until well combined but not smooth. Put into large non-metal bowl.

Add shrimp. Stir to coat well. Cover. Chill for at least 3 hours or overnight.

Alternate shrimp and both colours of peppers on skewers. Cook on greased electric grill over medium heat for about 3 minutes per side until shrimp are pink and peppers are tender-crisp. Makes 8 skewers.

1 skewer: 76 Calories; 4.4 g Total Fat (1.3 g Mono, 2 g Poly, 0.9 g Sat); 35 mg Cholesterol; 4 g Carbohydrate; 1 g Fibre; 6 g Protein; 59 mg Sodium

Pictured on page 17.

Note: Pepitas (pumpkin seeds with or without the hull removed) are available in the bulk section of grocery stores or health food stores.

Mussels In Basil Cream

Fresh mussels in a rich-tasting but surprisingly light sauce. A seafood lover's delight that is perfect for a special occasion.

Water		
Fresh (blue) mussels, scrubbed clean	3 lbs.	1.4 kg
Finely chopped onion	1/2 cup	125 mL
Garlic cloves, minced (or 1 tsp., 5 mL, powder)	4	4
Chili paste (sambal oelek)	1/2 – 1 tsp.	2 – 5 mL
Canola oil	2 tsp.	10 mL
All-purpose flour	1 tbsp.	15 mL
Dry white (or alcohol-free) wine	1/2 cup	125 mL
Milk	1 1/2 cups	375 mL
Dijon mustard	2 tsp.	10 mL
Pepper	1/2 tsp.	2 mL
Chopped fresh sweet basil (or 3 1/2 tsp., 17 mL, dried)	1/3 cup	75 mL

Put enough water into large pot or Dutch oven to reach 1/4 full. Bring to a boil on medium-high. Add mussels. Cover. Simmer for about 5 minutes until shells are opened and mussels are tender. Drain, reserving 1/2 cup (125 mL) broth. Turn mussels into medium bowl, discarding any that are unopened. Cover to keep warm.

Sauté onion, garlic and chili paste in canola oil in large frying pan on medium-high for about 5 minutes until onion is soft.

Sprinkle with flour. Heat and stir on medium for 1 minute to cook flour.

Add wine. Heat and stir until thickened.

Add milk, mustard, pepper and reserved broth. Heat and stir for about 10 minutes until slightly thickened.

Add basil. Stir. Add mussels. Stir to coat. Serves 4.

1 serving: 166 Calories; 5.8 g Total Fat (2.2 g Mono, 1.4 g Poly, 1.2 g Sat); 31 mg Cholesterol; 13 g Carbohydrate; 1 g Fibre; 16 g Protein; 411 mg Sodium

Bruschetta

The riper the tomatoes, the more delicious the bruschetta. If possible, use fresh basil for truly exquisite flavour. This is a perfect summertime appetizer. Follow this with Crunchy Vegetable Macaroni, page 113, and you have the perfect luncheon.

Finely chopped ripe roma (plum) tomato (about 6 medium)	**2 cups**	**500 mL**
Finely chopped red onion	**1/3 cup**	**75 mL**
Chopped fresh sweet basil (or 2 1/4 tsp., 11 mL, dried)	**3 tbsp.**	**50 mL**
Finely grated fresh Parmesan cheese	**2 tbsp.**	**30 mL**
Balsamic vinegar	**2 tbsp.**	**30 mL**
Olive (or canola) oil	**2 tsp.**	**10 mL**
Pepper	**1/2 tsp.**	**2 mL**
Multi-grain oval bread loaf, cut into 1 inch (2.5 cm) thick slices (see Note)	**1**	**1**
Garlic cloves, halved	**1 – 2**	**1 – 2**

Combine first 7 ingredients in medium non-metal bowl. Cover. Chill for at least 2 hours or overnight, stirring occasionally, to blend flavours.

Spray both sides of each bread slice with cooking spray. Lay bread slices on ungreased baking sheet. Bake in 350°F (175°C) oven for 12 to 15 minutes, turning once, until golden.

Rub cut side of garlic on both sides of each bread slice. Divide and spoon tomato mixture onto bread slices. Makes 16 appetizers.

1 appetizer: 67 Calories; 1.7 g Total Fat (0.8 g Mono, 0.3 g Poly, 0.4 g Sat); 1 mg Cholesterol; 11 g Carbohydrate; 2 g Fibre; 3 g Protein; 115 mg Sodium

Pictured on page 17.

Note: Country Seed Bread, page 39, can be used.

To toast coconut, nuts or seeds, place in single layer in ungreased shallow pan. Bake in 350°F (175°C) oven for 5 to 10 minutes, stirring or shaking often, until desired doneness.

Spiced Iced Tea

A thirst-quenching summer beverage with a citrus zing and a hint of cinnamon. Splash this attractive red refresher over ice and serve with a slice of lemon.

Raspberry herbal tea bags	**4**	**4**
Boiling water	**4 cups**	**1 L**
Strips of orange peel (4 inch, 10 cm, lengths)	**2**	**2**
Cinnamon stick (4 inch, 10 cm, length)	**1**	**1**
Star anise	**1**	**1**
Granulated sugar	**1/4 cup**	**60 mL**

Place tea bags in heatproof 1 quart (1 L) liquid measure. Pour boiling water over tea bags. Stir. Cover. Let steep for 2 to 5 minutes to desired strength. Squeeze and discard tea bags.

Add remaining 4 ingredients. Stir. Let stand for at least 30 minutes until desired spiciness is reached. Strain, discarding solids. Cover. Chill for about 3 hours until cold. Makes 4 cups (1 L).

1 cup (250 mL): 49 Calories; 0 g Total Fat (0 g Mono, 0 g Poly, 0 g Sat); 0 mg Cholesterol; 13 g Carbohydrate; 0 g Fibre; 0 g Protein; 2 mg Sodium

Pictured on page 72.

Wake-Up-Call Beverage

A little bit of tea, some protein and lots of fruit make this drink a healthy and delicious breakfast to have on the go. Instead of throwing away that last overripe banana, peel, slice and freeze it so you always have some on hand for this cool treat.

Vanilla soy milk	**1 cup**	**250 mL**
Green tea bags (fruit-flavoured or plain)	**2**	**2**
Ripe medium banana, cut into 1/2 inch (12 mm) slices, partially frozen	**1**	**1**
Frozen (or fresh) strawberries, cut into 1/2 inch (12 mm) slices, partially frozen	**1 cup**	**250 mL**
Liquid honey	**2 tbsp.**	**30 mL**

(continued on next page)

Heat and stir soy milk in small saucepan on high for about 4 minutes until boiling. Add tea bags. Cover. Let steep for 5 minutes. Squeeze and discard tea bags. Pour into 2 cup (500 mL) liquid measure. Chill.

Put banana and strawberries into blender. Add honey and tea mixture. Process until smooth. Makes 2 cups (500 mL).

1 cup (250 mL): 219 Calories; 3.6 g Total Fat (0.6 g Mono, 1.7 g Poly, 0.6 g Sat); 0 mg Cholesterol; 45 g Carbohydrate; 3 g Fibre; 5 g Protein; 71 mg Sodium

Pictured on page 36.

Pineapple Lemon Punch

This punch is both tart and sweet. The juicy chunks of pineapple really make this drink special so make sure you use one that is ripe. This will be a hit at any party or a great luncheon drink.

Pineapple juice	**1 cup**	**250 mL**
Freshly squeezed lemon juice (about 2 small lemons)	**1/2 cup**	**125 mL**
Granulated sugar	**1/2 cup**	**125 mL**
Club soda, chilled	**2 cups**	**500 mL**
Chopped fresh pineapple, 1/4 inch (6 mm) pieces (about 1/2 medium)	**2 cups**	**500 mL**

Stir pineapple juice, lemon juice and sugar in large pitcher until sugar is dissolved. Chill until cold.

Add club soda and pineapple. Stir. Makes about 5 1/2 cups (1.4 L).

1 cup (250 mL): 136 Calories; 0.2 g Total Fat (trace Mono, 0.1 g Poly, trace Sat); 0 mg Cholesterol; 35 g Carbohydrate; 1 g Fibre; trace Protein; 21 mg Sodium

Pictured on back cover.

Mango Smoothie

A thick and creamy treat with a tropical tang! Perfect for a light breakfast or a hot afternoon on the patio. Experiment with other favourite fruits such as strawberries, raspberries or blueberries.

Can of sliced mango in syrup, drained and 1/4 cup (60 mL) syrup reserved (or 1 cup, 250 mL, chopped fresh mango and 1/4 cup, 60 mL, pineapple juice)	**14 oz.**	**398 mL**
Low-fat vanilla yogurt	**1 cup**	**250 mL**
Prepared orange juice	**1 cup**	**250 mL**
Crushed ice	**1/2 cup**	**125 mL**

Put all 4 ingredients into blender with reserved syrup. Process until smooth. Makes about 3 1/4 cups (800 mL).

1 cup (250 mL): 150 Calories; 1.2 g Total Fat (0.3 g Mono, 0.1 g Poly, 0.7 g Sat); 4 mg Cholesterol; 32 g Carbohydrate; 1 g Fibre; 5 g Protein; 54 mg Sodium

Pictured on page 36.

Berry Smoothie

This sweet, smooth berry beverage will wake up your taste buds. A subtle hint of cinnamon and maple adds a delicate flavour to the drink. A berry lover's delight!

Milk	**1 1/2 cups**	**375 mL**
Frozen (or fresh) whole strawberries	**12**	**12**
Frozen (or fresh) whole raspberries	**2/3 cup**	**150 mL**
Frozen (or fresh) blackberries	**2/3 cup**	**150 mL**
Frozen low-fat strawberry yogurt	**1/2 cup**	**125 mL**
Maple (or maple-flavoured) syrup	**1/4 cup**	**60 mL**
Ground cinnamon	**1/2 tsp.**	**2 mL**

Put all 7 ingredients into blender. Process until smooth. Makes about 4 cups (1 L).

1 cup (250 mL): 163 Calories; 1.3 g Total Fat (0.2 g Mono, 0.2 g Poly, 0.6 g Sat); 6 mg Cholesterol; 34 g Carbohydrate; 4 g Fibre; 5 g Protein; 73 mg Sodium

Variation: Omit strawberries, raspberries and blackberries. Use about 2 2/3 cups (650 mL) frozen mixed berries.

Cherry Oat Muffins

The warm blend of spices and cherries makes these muffins a favourite. Great as a lunch box treat or afternoon snack.

Buttermilk (or reconstituted from powder)	2 cups	500 mL
Dried cherries, coarsely chopped	1 1/2 cups	375 mL
Rolled oats (not instant)	1 cup	250 mL
Large egg	1	1
Egg white (large)	1	1
Canola oil	2 tbsp.	30 mL
Finely grated lemon zest	1 tsp.	5 mL
Whole wheat flour	1 2/3 cups	400 mL
Baking powder	2 tsp.	10 mL
Baking soda	1 tsp.	5 mL
Commercial mixed spice	1/2 tsp.	2 mL
Brown sugar, packed	2/3 cup	150 mL
Granulated sugar	3 tbsp.	50 mL

Combine buttermilk, cherries and rolled oats in medium bowl. Cover. Let stand for 30 minutes. Stir.

Add next 4 ingredients. Mix well.

Combine next 5 ingredients in large bowl. Make a well in centre. Add rolled oat mixture. Stir until just moistened. Do not overmix.

Fill greased muffin cups 3/4 full. Sprinkle with granulated sugar. Bake in 375°F (190°C) oven for 20 to 25 minutes until wooden pick inserted in centre of muffin comes out clean. Let stand in pan for 5 minutes before turning out onto wire rack to cool completely. Makes 12 muffins.

1 muffin: 251 Calories; 3.9 g Total Fat (1.8 g Mono, 1.1 g Poly, 0.7 g Sat); 19 mg Cholesterol; 48 g Carbohydrate; 4 g Fibre; 7 g Protein; 252 mg Sodium

Low-fat and non-fat dairy products have less fat and calories but still provide the protein and calcium essential to healthy eating. Be sure to read the labels and choose products with a lower percent M.F. (milk fat) or B.F. (butter fat).

Pineapple Bran Muffins

Delicious muffins are packed with fruit and flavour. Serve for a quick breakfast or an afternoon snack.

All-bran cereal	**1 cup**	**250 mL**
All-purpose flour	**1 cup**	**250 mL**
Granulated sugar	**1/2 cup**	**125 mL**
Baking powder	**1 tsp.**	**5 mL**
Baking soda	**1/2 tsp.**	**2 mL**
Egg whites (large)	**2**	**2**
Canola oil	**1/4 cup**	**60 mL**
Low-fat vanilla yogurt	**2/3 cup**	**150 mL**
Can of crushed pineapple, well drained	**14 oz.**	**398 mL**

Stir first 5 ingredients in large bowl. Make a well in centre.

Beat egg whites, canola oil and yogurt in medium bowl until well mixed. Stir in pineapple. Pour into well. Stir until just moistened. Do not overmix. Let stand for about 10 minutes until cereal is softened. Fill greased muffin cups 3/4 full. Bake in 400°F (205°C) oven for about 15 minutes until wooden pick inserted in centre of muffin comes out clean. Let stand in pan for 5 minutes before turning out onto wire rack to cool completely. Makes 12 muffins.

1 muffin: 152 Calories; 5.1 g Total Fat (2.8 g Mono, 1.5 g Poly, 0.5 g Sat); 1 mg Cholesterol; 26 g Carbohydrate; 2 g Fibre; 3 g Protein; 113 mg Sodium

Pictured on page 18.

1. Greens And Fruit Salad, page 64
2. Baked Apple Breakfast, page 44
3. Chicken Spinach Frittata, page 51

Banana Ginger Muffins

A light-textured muffin with a warm banana taste. The hint of spicy ginger contrasts the sweet brown sugar topping.

All-purpose flour	1 1/2 cups	375 mL
Whole wheat flour	1/3 cup	75 mL
Baking powder	1 tbsp.	15 mL
Brown sugar, packed	1/2 cup	125 mL
Minced crystallized ginger	3 tbsp.	50 mL
Rolled oats (not instant)	1/2 cup	125 mL
Mashed banana (about 2 large)	1 cup	250 mL
Large egg, fork-beaten	1	1
Buttermilk (or reconstituted from powder)	1 1/4 cups	300 mL
Canola oil	2 tbsp.	30 mL
Maple (or maple-flavoured) syrup	1/4 cup	60 mL
Brown sugar, packed	3 tbsp.	50 mL

Combine first 6 ingredients in large bowl. Make a well in centre.

Mix next 5 ingredients in medium bowl. Pour into well. Stir until just moistened. Do not overmix.

Fill greased muffin cups 3/4 full. Sprinkle with second amount of brown sugar. Bake in 375°F (190°C) oven for 20 to 25 minutes until golden brown and wooden pick inserted in centre of muffin comes out clean. Let stand in pan for 5 minutes before turning out onto wire rack to cool completely. Makes 12 muffins.

1 muffin: 215 Calories; 3.5 g Total Fat (1.7 g Mono, 0.9 g Poly, 0.6 g Sat); 19 mg Cholesterol; 43 g Carbohydrate; 2 g Fibre; 4 g Protein; 164 mg Sodium

Pictured on page 36.

1. Wake-Up-Call Beverage, page 30
2. Mango Smoothie, page 32
3. Dressed-Up Fruit Cups, page 138
4. Banana Ginger Muffins, above

Peach Spice Muffins

A moist, light muffin with tender pieces of peach and a mild spice flavour. Can be served warm to bring out the spicy flavour.

All-purpose flour	1 cup	250 mL
Whole wheat flour	3/4 cup	175 mL
Baking powder	1 tbsp.	15 mL
Ground cinnamon	1/2 tsp.	2 mL
Ground ginger	1/2 tsp.	2 mL
Ground allspice	1/4 tsp.	1 mL
Dark brown sugar, packed	3/4 cup	175 mL
Can of peach halves in natural juice, drained, chopped	14 oz.	398 mL
Large egg	1	1
Buttermilk (or reconstituted from powder)	3/4 cup	175 mL
Apple juice	1/3 cup	75 mL
Canola oil	2 tbsp.	30 mL

Combine first 7 ingredients in large bowl. Make a well in centre.

Combine remaining 5 ingredients in medium bowl. Pour into well. Stir until just moistened. Do not overmix. Fill greased muffin cups 3/4 full. Bake in 375°F (190°C) oven for 20 to 25 minutes until wooden pick inserted in centre of muffin comes out clean. Let stand in pan for 5 minutes before turning out onto wire rack to cool completely. Makes 12 muffins.

1 muffin: 173 Calories; 3.2 g Total Fat (1.6 g Mono, 0.9 g Poly, 0.5 g Sat); 18 mg Cholesterol; 34 g Carbohydrate; 2 g Fibre; 4 g Protein; 153 mg Sodium

APRICOT SPICE MUFFINS: Omit peaches. Use same amount of apricots.

To reduce fat in your diet, spread less margarine or butter on bread, toast, buns, bagels and muffins. Measure out 1 tsp. (5 mL) rather than just scooping with your knife directly from the tub or block.

Country Seed Bread

A hearty, grainy loaf with a beautiful golden crust. The sunflower seeds and flaxseed give it a pleasing chewy texture. Delicious served with Split Pea Dip, page 26, or as the base for Bruschetta, page 29.

Milk	1 1/4 cups	300 mL
Multi-grain cereal (7-grain mix)	1/4 cup	60 mL
Tub margarine	2 tbsp.	30 mL
Brown sugar, packed	2 tbsp.	30 mL
Salt	1 1/4 tsp.	6 mL
Whole wheat flour	1 1/4 cups	300 mL
Instant yeast	1 tbsp.	15 mL
All-purpose flour	1 cup	250 mL
Raw unsalted sunflower seeds	3 tbsp.	50 mL
All-purpose flour, approximately	1/3 cup	75 mL
Egg white (large)	1	1
Water	1 tbsp.	15 mL
Multi-grain cereal (7-grain mix)	2 tsp.	10 mL
Flaxseed	1/2 tsp.	2 mL

Combine first 5 ingredients in small saucepan. Heat and stir on medium until almost boiling. Pour into large bowl. Let stand for 10 minutes. Mixture should still be warm.

Combine whole wheat flour and yeast in small bowl. Add to milk mixture. Beat until consistency of thick batter.

Stir in first amount of all-purpose flour and sunflower seeds until moistened.

Turn dough out onto floured surface. Knead for about 10 minutes, working in enough of second amount of all-purpose flour, until dough is smooth and elastic. Place dough in lightly greased large bowl, turning once to grease top. Cover with greased waxed paper and tea towel. Let stand in oven with light on and door closed for about 1 hour until doubled in bulk. Punch dough down. Divide into 2 portions. Shape each into loaf about 12 inches (30 cm) long. Place on greased baking sheets. Cover with greased waxed paper and tea towel. Let stand in oven with light on and door closed for 30 to 40 minutes until almost doubled in size.

Beat egg white and water with fork in small bowl until blended. Brush over dough.

Sprinkle with second amount of cereal and flaxseed. Make 3 diagonal slashes on top of each loaf with sharp knife. Bake in 375°F (190°C) oven for about 20 minutes until golden and hollow-sounding when tapped. Turn out onto wire racks to cool. Makes 2 loaves, each cutting into 16 slices, for a total of 32 slices.

1 slice: 56 Calories; 1 g Total Fat (0.3 g Mono, 0.5 g Poly, 0.2 g Sat); trace Cholesterol; 10 g Carbohydrate; 1 g Fibre; 2 g Protein; 96 mg Sodium

Pictured on page 17 and on page 108.

Whole Grain Bread

A wholesome loaf with a nutty taste. Serve warm from the oven or toast and spread with your favourite jam.

Bulgur	**1/2 cup**	**125 mL**
Buckwheat groats (or kasha)	**1/4 cup**	**60 mL**
Cracked rye	**1/4 cup**	**60 mL**
Boiling water, to cover		
Granulated sugar	**1 tsp.**	**5 mL**
Warm milk	**1 cup**	**250 mL**
Active dry yeast	**1 tbsp.**	**15 mL**
All-purpose flour	**2 cups**	**500 mL**
Whole wheat flour	**2/3 cup**	**150 mL**
Salt	**1/2 tsp.**	**2 mL**
Egg yolk (large)	**1**	**1**
Milk	**1 tsp.**	**5 mL**
Buckwheat groats (or kasha)	**1 tbsp.**	**15 mL**

Combine first 4 ingredients in medium bowl. Cover. Let stand for 30 minutes. Drain through sieve. Rinse under cold water. Drain well through sieve.

Stir sugar and first amount of milk in small bowl until dissolved. Sprinkle yeast over top. Let stand for 10 minutes. Stir to dissolve yeast.

Combine both flours and salt in large bowl. Add bulgur mixture. Mix well. Stir in yeast mixture. Mix until dough just comes together. Turn out onto lightly floured surface. Knead for 5 to 10 minutes until dough is smooth and elastic. Place dough in large greased bowl, turning once to grease top. Cover with greased waxed paper and tea towel. Let stand in oven with light on and door closed for about 1 hour until doubled in bulk. Punch dough down. Turn dough out onto lightly floured surface. Knead until smooth. Divide into 3 equal portions. Roll each out to form 12 inch (30 cm) long rolls. Press 3 ends together at top. Braid rolls together, pinching last 3 ends together. Place in greased 8 x 4 x 3 inch (20 x 10 x 7.5 cm) loaf pan. Cover with greased waxed paper and tea towel. Let stand in oven with light on and door closed for about 35 minutes until doubled in size.

(continued on next page)

Mix egg yolk and second amount of milk in small cup. Brush over braid.

Sprinkle with second amount of buckwheat. Bake in 375°F (190°C) oven for about 40 minutes until golden brown and hollow-sounding when tapped. Turn out onto wire rack to cool. Cuts into about 16 slices.

1 slice: 117 Calories; 0.9 g Total Fat (0.3 g Mono, 0.2 g Poly, 0.3 g Sat); 14 mg Cholesterol; 23 g Carbohydrate; 3 g Fibre; 5 g Protein; 70 mg Sodium

Pictured on page 18.

Chili Cornbread

Cornbread with a spicy twist. Great served with chilies, stews or soups. Enjoy warm from the oven.

All-purpose flour	1/2 cup	125 mL
Whole wheat flour	1/2 cup	125 mL
Baking powder	2 tsp.	10 mL
Yellow cornmeal	3/4 cup	175 mL
Granulated sugar	1/3 cup	75 mL
Ground cumin	1 tsp.	5 mL
Salt	1/4 tsp.	1 mL
Chopped fresh cilantro (or fresh parsley)	1 – 4 tbsp.	15 – 60 mL
Chopped fresh oregano (or 2 1/4 tsp., 11 mL, dried)	3 tbsp.	50 mL
Grated low-fat sharp Cheddar cheese	1/3 cup	75 mL
Buttermilk (or reconstituted from powder)	1 cup	250 mL
Chili paste (sambal oelek)	2 tsp.	10 mL
Large eggs, fork-beaten	3	3
Canola oil	3 tbsp.	50 mL
Can of cream-style corn (10 oz., 284 mL, size)	1/2	1/2

Combine first 10 ingredients in large bowl. Make a well in centre.

Combine remaining 5 ingredients in small bowl. Pour into well. Mix. Pour into well-greased 9 x 9 inch (22 x 22 cm) pan. Bake in 375°F (190°C) oven for about 1 hour until wooden pick inserted in centre comes out clean. Let stand in pan for 10 minutes before turning out onto wire rack. Serve warm or cool. Cuts into 9 to 12 pieces.

1 piece: 220 Calories; 8.1 g Total Fat (3.9 g Mono, 1.9 g Poly, 1.3 g Sat); 73 mg Cholesterol; 31 g Carbohydrate; 2 g Fibre; 7 g Protein; 311 mg Sodium

Pictured on page 53.

Whole Wheat Buns

Delicious golden buns with a crusty bottom and chewy centre. Sprinkle with your favourite seeds.

Granulated sugar	**1 tbsp.**	**15 mL**
Warm water	**1/2 cup**	**125 mL**
Warm milk	**1 cup**	**250 mL**
Active dry yeast (or 1/4 oz., 8 g, envelope)	**1 tbsp.**	**15 mL**
All-purpose flour	**1 1/2 cups**	**375 mL**
Whole wheat flour	**1 1/4 cups**	**300 mL**
Granulated sugar	**1 tbsp.**	**15 mL**
Salt	**2 tsp.**	**10 mL**
All-purpose flour, approximately	**1/2 cup**	**125 mL**
Egg yolk (large)	**1**	**1**
Water	**1 tsp.**	**5 mL**
Poppy (or sesame) seeds	**4 tsp.**	**20 mL**

Stir first amount of sugar into first amount of water and milk in small bowl until dissolved. Sprinkle yeast over top. Let stand for 10 minutes. Stir to dissolve yeast.

Combine next 4 ingredients in large bowl. Stir in yeast mixture. Mix until dough is just moistened.

Turn dough out onto lightly floured surface. Knead for 5 to 10 minutes, working in enough of second amount of all-purpose flour, until dough is smooth and elastic. Place dough in large greased bowl, turning once to grease top. Cover with greased plastic wrap and tea towel. Let stand in oven with light on and door closed for about 45 minutes until doubled in bulk. Turn dough out onto lightly floured surface. Knead until smooth. Divide into 12 portions. Roll or form each portion into bun shape. Arrange buns about 2 inches (5 cm) apart on greased baking sheet. Loosely cover with greased plastic wrap. Let stand in oven with light on and door closed for 20 to 25 minutes until doubled in size.

Combine egg yolk and second amount of water in separate small bowl. Brush over each bun.

Sprinkle with poppy seeds. Bake in 375°F (190°C) oven for about 20 minutes until golden brown. Turn out onto wire rack to cool completely. Makes 12 buns.

1 bun: 131 Calories; 1.4 g Total Fat (0.3 g Mono, 0.2 g Poly, 0.4 g Sat); 19 mg Cholesterol; 25 g Carbohydrate; 2 g Fibre; 5 g Protein; 407 mg Sodium

Pictured on page 18.

Pumpkin And Herb Biscuits

Light golden biscuits. Substitute the chives and thyme with a blend of your favourite herbs.

All-purpose flour	**1 1/2 cups**	**375 mL**
Whole wheat flour	**1/2 cup**	**125 mL**
Baking powder	**1 tbsp.**	**15 mL**
Chopped fresh chives (or 2 1/4 tsp., 11 mL, dried)	**3 tbsp.**	**50 mL**
Chopped fresh thyme (or 3/4 tsp., 4 mL, dried)	**1 tbsp.**	**15 mL**
Ground nutmeg	**1/2 tsp.**	**2 mL**
Salt	**1/2 tsp.**	**2 mL**
Pepper	**1/2 tsp.**	**2 mL**
Large egg	**1**	**1**
Canned pure pumpkin (no spices), see Note	**1/2 cup**	**125 mL**
Buttermilk (or reconstituted from powder)	**1/2 cup**	**125 mL**
Canola oil	**3 tbsp.**	**50 mL**
Large egg, fork-beaten	**1**	**1**

Combine first 8 ingredients in large bowl. Make a well in centre.

Beat first egg with fork in medium bowl. Add pumpkin, buttermilk and canola oil. Stir. Add to well. Mix until soft dough forms. Do not overmix. Turn dough out onto lightly floured surface. Press out to 1 inch (2.5 cm) thickness. Cut with 2 inch (5 cm) round cutter. Arrange, almost touching, in greased 9 x 9 inch (22 x 22 cm) pan.

Brush tops with second egg. Bake in 475°F (240°C) oven for 12 to 15 minutes until golden. Makes about 12 biscuits.

1 biscuit: 130 Calories; 5.1 g Total Fat (2.7 g Mono, 1.4 g Poly, 0.7 g Sat); 36 mg Cholesterol; 17 g Carbohydrate; 1 g Fibre; 4 g Protein; 225 mg Sodium

Pictured on page 71.

Note: Use a 14 oz., 398 mL, can. Freeze leftover pumpkin in 1/2 cup (125 mL) portions for future use in baking.

Baked Apple Breakfast

The inviting flavours of honey and cinnamon will make this a breakfast favourite.

Medium cooking apples (such as McIntosh), with peel, cored and thinly sliced	**4**	**4**
Diced dried figs	**1/4 cup**	**60 mL**
Prepared orange juice	**1/2 cup**	**125 mL**
Ground cinnamon	**1/2 tsp.**	**2 mL**
Liquid honey	**2 tbsp.**	**30 mL**
Granola with almonds cereal	**1/2 cup**	**125 mL**
Peach, passion fruit and mango (or apricot peach) spread	**1/4 cup**	**60 mL**
Liquid honey	**1 tbsp.**	**15 mL**

Lightly spray 2 quart (2 L) casserole with cooking spray. Spread apple in even layer. Scatter figs over apple.

Combine orange juice, cinnamon and first amount of honey in small bowl or cup. Pour over figs. Cover. Bake in 350°F (175°C) oven for about 30 minutes until apple is tender-crisp.

Sprinkle with cereal.

Microwave fruit spread and second amount of honey in small microwave-safe bowl on high (100%) for 15 to 20 seconds until pourable consistency. Drizzle over cereal. Bake, uncovered, for about 10 minutes until cereal is lightly browned. Serves 4.

1 serving: 304 Calories; 3.9 g Total Fat (1.2 g Mono, 0.9 g Poly, 0.5 g Sat); 0 mg Cholesterol; 70 g Carbohydrate; 6 g Fibre; 3 g Protein; 17 mg Sodium

Pictured on page 35.

An apple a day keeps the doctor away—especially when combined with other fruits, vegetables, whole grains, legumes and seafood!

Lemon Bran Scones

Poppy seeds and rolled oats give these golden scones a pleasing texture. You'll enjoy the hint of cinnamon and subtle zing of lemon. Serve for breakfast, afternoon tea or as a healthy snack.

All-purpose flour	1 cup	250 mL
Whole wheat flour	1/2 cup	125 mL
Rolled oats (not instant)	1/2 cup	125 mL
Natural wheat bran	1/4 cup	60 mL
Poppy seeds	2 tbsp.	30 mL
Baking powder	1 tbsp.	15 mL
Ground cinnamon	1/2 tsp.	2 mL
Salt	1/4 tsp.	1 mL
Large egg	1	1
Canola oil	1/4 cup	60 mL
Granulated sugar	1/3 cup	75 mL
Finely grated lemon zest	2 tsp.	10 mL
Buttermilk (or reconstituted from powder)	2/3 cup	150 mL
TOPPING		
Milk	2 tsp.	10 mL
Granulated sugar	1/2 tbsp.	7 mL

Combine first 8 ingredients in large bowl. Make a well in centre.

Mix next 5 ingredients in small bowl. Pour into well. Mix until soft, sticky dough forms. Do not overmix. Drop by rounded tablespoonfuls, about 2 inches (5 cm) apart, onto greased baking sheet.

Topping: Brush tops with milk. Sprinkle with sugar. Bake in 400°F (205°C) oven for about 10 minutes until lightly browned. Makes about 2 dozen scones.

1 scone: 78 Calories; 3.1 g Total Fat (1.5 g Mono, 0.8 g Poly, 0.3 g Sat); 9 mg Cholesterol; 11 g Carbohydrate; 1 g Fibre; 2 g Protein; 92 mg Sodium

Drink nutrition-packed fresh fruit or vegetable juice instead of soft drinks or caffeinated beverages that have no nutritional value.

Breakfast Quiche

The savoury combination of tangy tomatoes, earthy mushrooms, mild Swiss cheese and sweet herbs will make this dish a favourite. Attractive and easy enough to prepare for brunch guests.

Natural oat bran	2 tbsp.	30 mL
Grated light Swiss cheese	1/2 cup	125 mL
Sliced fresh mushrooms	1 1/2 cups	375 mL
Pepper, sprinkle		
Green onions, sliced	3	3
Medium roma (plum) tomatoes, diced	2	2
Package of frozen egg product, thawed (see Note)	8 oz.	227 mL
Soft tofu	2/3 cup	150 mL
Evaporated skim milk	1/2 cup	125 mL
Grated light Swiss cheese	1/2 cup	125 mL
All-purpose flour	1 tbsp.	15 mL
Dried sweet basil	1/4 tsp.	1 mL
Garlic powder	1/4 tsp.	1 mL
Paprika, sprinkle		
Chopped fresh dill (or 1/2 tsp., 2 mL, dill weed)	2 tsp.	10 mL

Spray 9 inch (22 cm) pie plate with cooking spray. Sprinkle with oat bran. Sprinkle first amount of Swiss cheese evenly over oat bran. Set aside.

Cook mushrooms and pepper in large non-stick frying pan on medium-high for about 5 minutes, stirring occasionally, until golden.

Add green onion. Stir-fry for 1 minute. Scatter evenly over cheese. Sprinkle with tomato.

Put next 7 ingredients into blender. Process until smooth. Slowly pour over tomato, allowing spaces to fill in with liquid.

Sprinkle with paprika and dill. Bake, uncovered, in 375°F (190°C) oven for about 35 minutes until set. Let stand in pie plate for 5 minutes before cutting. Cuts into 6 wedges.

1 wedge: 117 Calories; 2.5 g Total Fat (0.7 g Mono, 0.6 g Poly, 0.9 g Sat); 9 mg Cholesterol; 9 g Carbohydrate; 2 g Fibre; 14 g Protein; 173 mg Sodium

Note: 3 tbsp. (50 mL) frozen egg product = 1 large egg.

Buckwheat Pancakes

There are pancakes and then there are these delicious buckwheat pancakes! These wholesome, satisfying breakfast treats will be a big hit. Serve with warm maple (or maple-flavoured) syrup and stewed peaches or apples. Look for buckwheat flour in grocery or health food stores.

Buckwheat flour	**1 cup**	**250 mL**
All-purpose flour	**1 cup**	**250 mL**
Granulated sugar	**2 tbsp.**	**30 mL**
Baking soda	**1 tsp.**	**5 mL**
Ground cinnamon	**1/4 tsp.**	**1 mL**
Ground nutmeg	**1/4 tsp.**	**1 mL**
Frozen egg product, thawed (see Note)	**1/2 cup**	**125 mL**
Apple juice	**1 cup**	**250 mL**
Canola oil	**1 tbsp.**	**15 mL**
Vanilla	**1/2 tsp.**	**2 mL**

Combine first 6 ingredients in medium bowl. Mix well. Make a well in centre.

Beat egg product in small bowl until light and fluffy. Add apple juice, canola oil and vanilla. Stir. Pour into well. Stir until thoroughly combined. For each pancake, spoon 1/4 cup (60 mL) batter onto hot lightly greased griddle or frying pan. Cook for about 2 minutes until bubbles appear on surface and bottom is golden. Turn over. Cook until lightly browned. Makes about ten 4 inch (10 cm) pancakes.

2 pancakes: 259 Calories; 4 g Total Fat (1.7 g Mono, 0.9 g Poly, 0.3 g Sat); 0 mg Cholesterol; 49 g Carbohydrate; 3 g Fibre; 9 g Protein; 310 mg Sodium

Note: 3 tbsp. (50 mL) frozen egg product = 1 large egg.

Eat a piece of fruit with every meal—fruit is a quick, convenient and nutritious dessert. Fruit is also great for snacking. Experiment with various fruits, such as star fruit, kumquats and papaya, for a fun, different treat.

Breakfast Couscous

A filling breakfast cereal that is ready in a flash. You will enjoy the variety of tastes and textures. The raisins and dates are sweet and chewy, the cranberries are tart and the almonds are crunchy.

Water	**1 cup**	**250 mL**
Couscous	**1 cup**	**250 mL**
Finely grated orange zest	**1/2 tsp.**	**2 mL**
Golden raisins	**1/2 cup**	**125 mL**
Dried cranberries	**1/2 cup**	**125 mL**
Chopped seeded dates	**1/2 cup**	**125 mL**
Slivered almonds, toasted (see Tip, page 29)	**1/4 cup**	**60 mL**
Milk	**1 cup**	**250 mL**
Low-fat plain yogurt	**1/3 cup**	**75 mL**
Brown sugar, packed	**2 tbsp.**	**30 mL**

Put water into medium saucepan. Bring to a boil. Add couscous and orange zest. Stir. Remove from heat. Cover. Let stand for about 5 minutes until liquid is absorbed. Fluff with fork.

Add remaining 7 ingredients. Stir. Makes about 4 cups (1 L).

1/2 cup (125 mL): 237 Calories; 2.8 g Total Fat (1.5 g Mono, 0.6 g Poly, 0.5 g Sat); 2 mg Cholesterol; 48 g Carbohydrate; 3 g Fibre; 6 g Protein; 30 mg Sodium

Many fruits are good sources of fibre and vitamins A and C. Don't forget to eat fruits that are high in folate (a B vitamin), such as strawberries, kiwifruit and papaya.

Mushroom And Herb Pie

A fabulous, crustless quiche with a rich mushroom flavour and a nip of cheese. This pie cuts beautifully. Best served warm.

Chicken Stock, page 12 (or Vegetable Stock, page 14)	**1/4 cup**	**60 mL**
Small fresh mushrooms, sliced	**6 cups**	**1.5 L**
Large eggs	**4**	**4**
Skim evaporated milk	**1/2 cup**	**125 mL**
Grated low-fat sharp Cheddar cheese	**1/4 cup**	**60 mL**
Chopped fresh chives (or 2 1/4 tsp., 11 mL, dried)	**3 tbsp.**	**50 mL**
Chopped fresh parsley (or 2 1/4 tsp., 11 mL, flakes)	**3 tbsp.**	**50 mL**
Pepper	**1/8 tsp.**	**0.5 mL**

Heat stock in large frying pan on medium-high. Add mushrooms. Cook for about 10 minutes until no liquid remains. Reserve 8 mushroom slices. Finely chop remaining mushrooms.

Beat eggs with fork in medium bowl. Add chopped mushrooms and remaining 5 ingredients. Stir. Pour into greased 9 inch (22 cm) pie plate. Arrange reserved mushroom slices around outer edge of mushroom mixture. Place pie plate in casserole large enough to hold it. Carefully pour enough boiling water into casserole so water reaches halfway up side of pie plate. Bake in 350°F (175°C) oven for about 30 minutes until set. Cuts into 6 wedges.

1 wedge: 99 Calories; 4.3 g Total Fat (1.5 g Mono, 0.6 g Poly, 1.4 g Sat); 143 mg Cholesterol; 6 g Carbohydrate; 1 g Fibre; 9 g Protein; 101 mg Sodium

Keep a daily food diary to track what you eat and when. This journal will help identify things to improve upon once you compare it to Canada's Food Guide.

Grilled Vegetable Pitas

You'll enjoy the crispiness of these light and delicious grilled pitas with the soft vegetable filling.

Low-fat plain yogurt	1/2 cup	125 mL
Chopped fresh mint leaves (or 1 tsp. – 1 tbsp., 5 – 15 mL, dried)	1 – 4 tbsp.	15 – 60 mL
Medium red peppers, quartered	2	2
Medium eggplant, cut into 1/4 inch (6 mm) thick slices	1	1
Medium zucchini, with peel, cut lengthwise into 1/4 inch (6 mm) thick slices	2	2
Red wine vinegar	1 tbsp.	15 mL
Liquid honey	1 tbsp.	15 mL
Olive (or canola) oil	2 tsp.	10 mL
Ground cumin	1/2 tsp.	2 mL
Coarsely ground pepper	1/4 tsp.	1 mL
Garlic cloves, minced (or 1/2 tsp., 2 mL, powder)	2	2
Whole wheat pita breads (about 6 inches, 15 cm)	4	4

Combine yogurt and mint in small bowl. Cover. Chill until ready to use.

Cook red peppers on greased electric grill over medium heat for about 10 minutes until skins are blistered and blackened. Place in medium bowl. Cover with plastic wrap. Let sweat for about 10 minutes until cool enough to handle. Peel and discard skin and seeds from peppers. Cut into 1/3 inch (1 cm) thick strips. Put into large bowl.

Lightly spray both sides of eggplant and zucchini slices with cooking spray. Cook on greased grill over medium heat for about 5 minutes per side until browned. Chop. Add to red pepper.

Combine next 6 ingredients in jar with tight-fitting lid. Shake well. Drizzle over vegetable mixture. Toss to coat well.

Make slit in seam of pitas to create opening. Gently ease knife into opening to separate layers without cutting all the way through. Spread 1/4 of yogurt mixture inside each. Divide and spoon vegetable mixture into each. Lightly spray cooking spray over pita pockets. Cook on greased grill over medium heat for 3 to 5 minutes per side until lightly browned. Makes 4 pita pockets.

1 pita pocket: 301 Calories; 5.6 g Total Fat (2.5 g Mono, 1.4 g Poly, 0.8 g Sat); 1 mg Cholesterol; 57 g Carbohydrate; 11 g Fibre; 11 g Protein; 375 mg Sodium

VEGETABLE PITAS: Broil for same amount of time rather than grill.

Chicken Spinach Frittata

This combination of chicken, spinach and cheese makes for an attractive, delicious dish. Serve hot or cold with a crisp garden salad.

Frozen egg product, thawed (see Note)	1 1/2 cups	375 mL
Chopped fresh chives (or 1 tbsp., 15 mL, dried)	1/4 cup	60 mL
Milk	1 tbsp.	15 mL
Medium leek (white and tender parts only), thinly sliced	1	1
Finely chopped yellow pepper	2/3 cup	150 mL
Olive (or canola) oil	2 tsp.	10 mL
Box of frozen spinach, thawed and squeezed dry	10 oz.	300 g
Chopped cooked chicken	1 1/2 cups	375 mL
Frozen peas	1/2 cup	125 mL
Grated Gruyère (or Swiss) cheese	1/4 cup	60 mL

Whisk egg product, chives and milk in large bowl. Set aside.

Sauté leek and yellow pepper in olive oil in large frying pan for 8 to 10 minutes, stirring occasionally, until leek is tender. Cool. Add to egg mixture. Stir.

Add spinach, chicken and peas. Stir. Pour into greased large frying pan. Press or spread evenly. Cook on medium for 5 to 7 minutes, without stirring, until frittata is set around edge.

Sprinkle with cheese. Cover. Reduce heat to medium-low. Cook for 5 to 7 minutes until set. Do not stir. Remove from heat. Do not remove cover. Let stand for 5 minutes. Cuts into 8 wedges.

1 wedge: 119 Calories; 3.2 g Total Fat (1.3 g Mono, 0.7 g Poly, 1 g Sat); 25 mg Cholesterol; 7 g Carbohydrate; 2 g Fibre; 16 g Protein; 167 mg Sodium

Pictured on page 35.

Note: 3 tbsp. (50 mL) frozen egg product = 1 large egg.

Creamy Turkey Wraps

A chunky turkey salad with the added crunch of celery and almonds. A creative way to use leftover turkey. Makes a healthy lunch.

Light sour cream	1/3 cup	75 mL
Whole cranberry sauce	3 tbsp.	50 mL
Prepared orange juice	3 tbsp.	50 mL
Chopped cooked turkey	1 1/2 cups	375 mL
Finely chopped celery	1/2 cup	125 mL
Green onions, finely chopped	4	4
Slivered almonds (optional), toasted (see Tip, page 29)	1/4 cup	60 mL
Large flour tortillas (about 10 inches, 25 cm)	4	4

Combine sour cream, cranberry sauce and orange juice in large bowl.

Add next 4 ingredients. Mix well.

Spoon about 2/3 cup (150 mL) mixture down centre of each tortilla. Roll up to enclose filling. Makes 4 wraps.

1 wrap: 374 Calories; 7.1 g Total Fat (2.8 g Mono, 0.9 g Poly, 2.6 g Sat); 52 mg Cholesterol; 51 g Carbohydrate; 4 g Fibre; 24 g Protein; 408 mg Sodium

CREAMY CHICKEN WRAPS: Omit turkey. Use same amount of chopped cooked chicken.

1. Chili Cornbread, page 41
2. Seafood Stew, page 93
3. Chicken Stew, page 87

Tuna Salad Sandwiches

Toasted almonds, red peppers and celery give this tuna filling an appetizing crunch. Also good on rye or whole wheat bread. A classic lunchtime favourite.

Can of flaked white tuna, packed in water, drained	**6 oz.**	**170 g**
Chopped green onion	**1/3 cup**	**75 mL**
Finely chopped red pepper	**1/3 cup**	**75 mL**
Finely chopped celery	**1/4 cup**	**60 mL**
Chopped fresh parsley (or 1 1/2 tsp., 7 mL, flakes)	**2 tbsp.**	**30 mL**
Ultra low-fat mayonnaise	**3 tbsp.**	**50 mL**
Lemon juice	**2 tsp.**	**10 mL**
Pepper	**1/4 tsp.**	**1 mL**
Multi-grain rolls, cut in half	**3**	**3**
Sliced almonds (optional), toasted (see Tip, page 29)	**3 tbsp.**	**50 mL**

Combine first 8 ingredients in medium bowl. Mix well.

Divide and spread tuna mixture onto bottom half of each roll. Sprinkle with almonds. Cover with top half of each roll. Makes 3 sandwiches.

1 sandwich: 279 Calories; 5.8 g Total Fat (2.2 g Mono, 1.3 g Poly, 1.2 g Sat); 26 mg Cholesterol; 34 g Carbohydrate; 5 g Fibre; 21 g Protein; 644 mg Sodium

Pictured on page 54.

1. Tuna Salad Sandwiches, above
2. Shrimp And Red Pepper Pizza, page 92
3. Couscous And Bean Salad, page 63

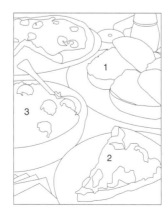

Shrimp And Rice Salad

This fresh salad is filled with scrumptious shrimp and drizzled with a zingy mango dressing. You can prepare this the day ahead and toss with dressing just before serving. A great barbecue salad!

Raw large shrimp	1 lb.	454 g
Boiling water	10 cups	2.5 L
Garlic cloves, minced (or 1/2 tsp., 2 mL, powder)	2	2
Curry powder	1 tbsp.	15 mL
Olive (or canola) oil	2 tsp.	10 mL
Cooked brown rice (1 1/3 cups, 325 mL, uncooked)	4 cups	1 L
Chopped tart cooking apple (such as Granny Smith), with peel	2 cups	500 mL
Chopped celery	1 cup	250 mL
Chopped red pepper	1 cup	250 mL
Chopped green onion	3/4 cup	175 mL
Chopped fresh parsley (or 2 tbsp., 30 mL, flakes)	1/2 cup	125 mL
Cashews (optional), toasted (see Tip, page 29) and coarsely chopped	1/3 cup	75 mL
MANGO DRESSING		
Can of sliced mango in syrup, drained	14 oz.	398 mL
Prepared orange juice	1/2 cup	125 mL
White wine vinegar	1/4 cup	60 mL
Olive (or canola) oil	1 tbsp.	15 mL
Granulated sugar	2 tsp.	10 mL
Ground cinnamon	1/2 tsp.	2 mL
Ground ginger	1/2 tsp.	2 mL

Cook shrimp in boiling water in large pot or Dutch oven for 2 to 3 minutes until pink and curled. Drain. Rinse under cold water. Peel and devein shrimp. Put into large bowl.

Sauté garlic and curry powder in olive oil in small frying pan for 1 to 2 minutes until fragrant. Add to shrimp.

Add next 7 ingredients. Toss.

Mango Dressing: Put all 7 ingredients into blender or food processor. Process until smooth. Makes 1 2/3 cups (400 mL) dressing. Drizzle over rice mixture. Toss. Makes 8 cups (2 L).

1 cup (250 mL): 248 Calories; 4.5 g Total Fat (2.5 g Mono, 0.8 g Poly, 0.7 g Sat); 67 mg Cholesterol; 42 g Carbohydrate; 5 g Fibre; 11 g Protein; 101 mg Sodium

Lettuce Parcels

A tantalizing mix of crunchy garden vegetables and chewy wheat berries rolled up in a leaf of crispy lettuce.

FILLING		
Wheat berries (unprocessed wheat kernels)	1/2 cup	125 mL
Cold water, to cover		
Vegetable Stock, page 14	3 cups	750 mL
Cinnamon stick (4 inch, 10 cm, length)	1	1
Whole green cardamom, bruised	6	6
(see Tip, page 103)		
Bay leaf	1	1
Dried crushed chilies (optional)	1/4 tsp.	1 mL
Chopped onion	1 cup	250 mL
Garlic cloves, minced (or 1/2 tsp., 2 mL, powder),	2	2
optional		
Canola oil	2 tsp.	10 mL
Chopped fresh bean sprouts	1 cup	250 mL
Finely chopped red cabbage	1/2 cup	125 mL
Grated carrot	1/3 cup	75 mL
Finely chopped red pepper	1/4 cup	60 mL
Green onion, thinly sliced	1	1
Chopped fresh parsley (or cilantro) or 2 1/4 tsp.	3 tbsp.	50 mL
(11 mL) flakes		
Non-fat Mediterranean-style dressing	1/4 cup	60 mL
Large iceberg (or green leaf) lettuce leaves	24	24

Filling: Heat and stir wheat in large non-stick frying pan on medium-high for 4 to 5 minutes until toasted. Transfer to medium bowl. Cover in cold water. Let stand for 4 hours or overnight. Drain. Put wheat into medium saucepan.

Add next 5 ingredients. Bring to a boil. Reduce heat to medium-low. Cover. Simmer for about 20 minutes, stirring occasionally, until wheat is tender and chewy. Harder varieties of wheat can take considerably longer to cook. Remove from heat. Drain. Cool. Remove and discard cinnamon, cardamom and bay leaf.

Sauté onion and garlic in canola oil in frying pan, stirring frequently, until onion is soft. Remove from heat.

Add wheat mixture and next 7 ingredients. Mix well. Makes 4 cups (1 L) filling.

Spoon about 2 1/2 tbsp. (37 mL) filling onto each lettuce leaf. Fold in sides. Roll up to enclose filling. Makes 24 lettuce parcels.

4 lettuce parcels: 86 Calories; 2.1 g Total Fat (1 g Mono, 0.6 g Poly, 0.2 g Sat); 0 mg Cholesterol; 15 g Carbohydrate; 3 g Fibre; 3 g Protein; 142 mg Sodium

Spinach Yam Salad

A unique and attractive salad that will bring words of praise from your guests. An interesting mix of fresh spinach, sweet yams and navy beans tossed in a balsamic and thyme dressing.

Small yam (or sweet potato), cut into 1/2 inch (12 mm) cubes (about 2 1/2 cups, 625 mL)	**1**	**1**
Pepper	**1/4 tsp.**	**1 mL**
Ground cinnamon	**1/2 tsp.**	**2 mL**
Bag of baby spinach leaves, stems removed	**6 oz.**	**170 g**
Slivered almonds, toasted (see Tip, page 29)	**1/4 cup**	**60 mL**
Navy Beans, page 19	**1 cup**	**250 mL**
DRESSING		
Finely grated orange zest	**1/2 tsp.**	**2 mL**
Freshly squeezed (or prepared) orange juice (about 1 medium orange)	**1/3 cup**	**75 mL**
Balsamic vinegar	**3 tbsp.**	**50 mL**
Olive (or canola) oil	**1 tbsp.**	**15 mL**
Chopped fresh thyme leaves (or 1/2 – 3/4 tsp., 2 – 4 mL, dried)	**1/2 – 1 tbsp.**	**7 – 15 mL**
Brown sugar, packed	**2 tsp.**	**10 mL**
Garlic clove, minced (or 1/4 tsp., 1 mL, powder)	**1**	**1**

Arrange yam on lightly greased baking sheet. Sprinkle with pepper and cinnamon. Toss. Spray with cooking spray. Bake in 375°F (190°C) oven for about 30 minutes, stirring occasionally, until softened and browned. Cool. Put into large bowl.

Add spinach, almonds and navy beans. Toss gently.

Dressing: Combine all 7 ingredients in jar with tight-fitting lid. Shake well. Makes about 1/2 cup (125 mL) dressing. Drizzle over yam mixture. Toss gently. Makes about 6 cups (1.5 L).

1 cup (250 mL): 165 Calories; 6 g Total Fat (3.8 g Mono, 1.1 g Poly, 0.6 g Sat); 0 mg Cholesterol; 24 g Carbohydrate; 5 g Fibre; 6 g Protein; 34 mg Sodium

Potato Pepper Salad

Savoury artichokes and roasted red peppers give this potato salad a unique and pleasing flavour. The sweet, citrus dressing will bring your guests back for seconds.

Red baby potatoes, halved (about 14)	**1 lb.**	**454 g**
Water		
Medium red peppers, quartered	**2**	**2**
Chopped green onion (about 4)	**1/2 cup**	**125 mL**
Can of artichoke hearts, drained, quartered	**14 oz.**	**398 mL**
DRESSING		
Prepared orange juice	**1/4 cup**	**60 mL**
White wine vinegar	**3 tbsp.**	**50 mL**
Chopped fresh sweet basil (or 3/4 – 2 1/4 tsp., 4 – 11 mL, dried)	**1 – 3 tbsp.**	**15 – 50 mL**
Olive (or cooking) oil	**1 tbsp.**	**15 mL**
Garlic clove, minced (or 1/4 tsp., 1 mL, powder)	**1**	**1**

Simmer potato in water in large saucepan on medium-low for about 15 minutes until tender but not mushy. Drain. Rinse under cold running water. Drain well.

Arrange red peppers, skin-side up, on baking sheet. Broil 4 inches (10 cm) from heat for about 10 minutes until skin is blistered and blackened. Put into small bowl. Cover with plastic wrap. Let sweat for about 10 minutes until cool enough to handle. Peel and discard skin and seeds from peppers. Cut peppers into 1/4 inch (6 mm) thick strips.

Combine potato, red pepper, green onion and artichoke in large bowl. Toss.

Dressing: Combine all 5 ingredients in jar with tight-fitting lid. Shake well. Makes 3/4 cup (175 mL) dressing. Drizzle over potato mixture. Toss. Makes 6 cups (1.5 L).

1 cup (250 mL): 82 Calories; 2.4 g Total Fat (1.7 g Mono, 0.2 g Poly, 0.3 g Sat); 0 mg Cholesterol; 13 g Carbohydrate; 5 g Fibre; 3 g Protein; 204 mg Sodium

Pictured on page 72.

Seafood Shells Vinaigrette

Succulent shrimp, scallops and colourful vegetables tossed with a seafood vinaigrette dressing. Serve on a bed of torn lettuce for a beautiful lunch salad. Double for a buffet or potluck salad.

VINAIGRETTE DRESSING		
White wine vinegar	2 tbsp.	30 mL
Water	2 tbsp.	30 mL
Lemon juice	2 tbsp.	30 mL
Grated lemon peel	1/2 tsp.	2 mL
Pectin crystals (see Note)	2 tsp.	10 mL
Seafood cocktail sauce	2 tbsp.	30 mL
Garlic clove, minced (or 1/4 tsp., 1 mL, powder)	1	1
Granulated sugar	1/2 tsp.	2 mL
Large shell pasta (not jumbo), about 1 1/2 cups (375 mL)	4 oz.	113 g
Boiling water	8 cups	2 L
White (or alcohol-free) wine	1/4 cup	60 mL
Water	1/4 cup	60 mL
Bay leaf	1	1
Fresh raw (or frozen, thawed) medium shrimp, peeled and deveined (about 6)	2 oz.	57 g
Fresh (or frozen, thawed) large sea scallops (about 3)	2 oz.	57 g
Small broccoli florets	1 1/2 cups	375 mL
Diced red pepper	2/3 cup	150 mL
Diced yellow pepper	2/3 cup	150 mL
Water		

Vinaigrette Dressing: Process first 8 ingredients in blender until smooth. Let stand for at least 20 minutes to blend flavours. Makes about 1/2 cup (125 mL) dressing.

Cook pasta in boiling water in large uncovered pot or Dutch oven for 10 to 12 minutes, stirring occasionally, until tender but firm. Drain. Rinse under cold water until cool. Drain. Transfer to large bowl.

Combine wine, water and bay leaf in small saucepan. Heat on medium-low until simmering.

Butterfly shrimp by cutting slightly deeper in cut made by deveining, but not quite through. When cooked, backs will open up and curl outward slightly. Add to wine mixture. Cover. Cook for about 1 1/2 minutes until shrimp are just pink and curled. Remove shrimp with slotted spoon to pasta.

(continued on next page)

Slice scallops in half horizontally. Add to wine mixture. Cover. Cook for about 2 minutes until scallops are opaque and firm. Do not overcook. Strain, discarding liquid and bay leaf. Add to pasta. Cover. Chill.

Cook broccoli and red and yellow pepper in water in medium saucepan for about 5 minutes until tender-crisp. Rinse under cold water until cool. Drain well. Add to pasta mixture. Drizzle dressing over pasta mixture. Toss. Makes about 4 1/2 cups (1.1 L).

1 cup (250 mL): 158 Calories; 0.9 g Total Fat (0.1 g Mono, 0.5 g Poly, 0.2 g Sat); 18 mg Cholesterol; 28 g Carbohydrate; 2 g Fibre; 8 g Protein; 144 mg Sodium

Pictured on front cover and on page 107.

Note: The addition of pectin crystals to a vinegar-based dressing achieves about the same viscosity as if oil had been added.

Variation: For easier and faster preparation, omit wine mixture and raw shrimp and scallops. Use 1 can (4 oz., 113 g) cooked salad shrimp, well drained.

Spinach Raspberry Salad

The tender, green spinach is complemented perfectly by the juicy, red raspberries, mild mushrooms and crunchy toasted almonds. This is a beautiful summer salad.

Bag of baby spinach leaves	**6 oz.**	**170 g**
Fresh raspberries	**1 1/3 cups**	**325 mL**
Thinly sliced fresh mushrooms	**1 cup**	**250 mL**
Sliced almonds, with skin, toasted (see Tip, page 29)	**1/3 cup**	**75 mL**
RASPBERRY VINAIGRETTE		
Raspberry vinegar (or red wine vinegar)	**3 tbsp.**	**50 mL**
Olive (or canola) oil	**1 tbsp.**	**15 mL**
Granulated sugar	**1 tsp.**	**5 mL**
Dijon mustard	**1 tsp.**	**5 mL**
Pepper	**1/4 tsp.**	**1 mL**

Combine first 4 ingredients in large bowl, reserving 4 raspberries.

Raspberry Vinaigrette: Put all 5 ingredients into blender. Add reserved raspberries. Process until smooth. Makes about 1/2 cup (125 mL) vinaigrette. Drizzle over spinach mixture. Toss. Makes about 8 cups (2 L).

1 cup (250 mL): 57 Calories; 3.9 g Total Fat (2.5 g Mono, 0.7 g Poly, 0.4 g Sat); 0 mg Cholesterol; 5 g Carbohydrate; 3 g Fibre; 2 g Protein; 33 mg Sodium

Pictured on page 89.

Lebanese Fattoush Salad

Tomatoes, cucumbers, olives and parsley give this herbaceous salad a wonderful mix of textures. The mint adds a distinct Lebanese flair.

DRESSING

Chicken Stock, page 12, chilled	1/4 cup	60 mL
White wine vinegar	1/4 cup	60 mL
Lemon juice	1/4 cup	60 mL
Olive (or canola) oil	2 tbsp.	30 mL
Granulated sugar	1/2 tsp.	2 mL
Cayenne pepper	1/16 tsp.	0.5 mL
Diced ripe tomato	1 1/2 cups	375 mL
Diced English cucumber, with peel	1 1/2 cups	375 mL
Can of sliced ripe olives, drained (about 1/4 cup, 60 mL), optional	7 oz.	200 mL
Finely chopped fresh parsley (or 2 tbsp., 30 mL, flakes)	1/2 cup	125 mL
Finely chopped fresh mint leaves (or 3 1/2 tsp. – 2 tbsp., 17 – 30 mL, dried)	1/3 – 1/2 cup	75 – 125 mL
Whole wheat pita breads (about 6 inches, 15 cm)	2	2
Chopped romaine lettuce hearts (about 2 small)	6 cups	1.5 L

Dressing: Combine first 6 ingredients in small jar with tight-fitting lid. Shake well until sugar is dissolved. Makes about 3/4 cup (175 mL) dressing.

Combine next 5 ingredients in large bowl. Drizzle dressing over tomato mixture. Toss. Marinate in refrigerator for 1 hour.

Arrange pitas in single layer on ungreased baking sheet. Bake in 350°F (175°C) oven for about 10 minutes until crisp. Cool completely. Break into bite-size pieces.

Add lettuce and pita to tomato mixture just before serving. Toss well. Makes 12 cups (3 L).

1 cup (250 mL): 65 Calories; 2.8 g Total Fat (1.8 g Mono, 0.4 g Poly, 0.3 g Sat); trace Cholesterol; 9 g Carbohydrate; 2 g Fibre; 2 g Protein; 64 mg Sodium

Pictured on page 72.

Couscous And Bean Salad

Couscous tossed with green beans and plump, red cherry tomatoes in a zesty dressing of honey, mustard and lemon. This is a healthy, summery salad that is very easy to prepare.

Chicken Stock, page 12 (or water)	2 cups	500 mL
Couscous	2 cups	500 mL
Water	6 cups	1.5 L
Fresh whole green beans, trimmed	3/4 lb.	340 g
Ice water		
Chickpeas, page 15	1 cup	250 mL
Thinly sliced red onion	1 cup	250 mL
Cherry (or grape) tomatoes, halved	2 cups	500 mL
Chopped fresh sweet basil (or 3/4 – 3 1/2 tsp., 4 – 17 mL, dried)	1 – 5 tbsp.	15 – 75 mL
LEMON MUSTARD DRESSING		
Finely grated lemon zest	1 tsp.	5 mL
Lemon juice (fresh is best)	1/2 – 2/3 cup	125 – 150 mL
Liquid honey	1/4 cup	60 mL
Grainy mustard	2 tbsp.	30 mL
Olive (or canola) oil	2 tbsp.	30 mL
Ground cumin (optional)	1/4 – 1 tsp.	1 – 5 mL
Pepper	1/4 tsp.	1 mL

Measure stock into medium saucepan. Bring to a boil. Add couscous. Stir. Remove from heat. Cover. Let stand for 5 minutes. Fluff with fork.

Measure water into large saucepan. Bring to a boil. Add green beans. Boil for 2 to 3 minutes until bright green. Drain. Place in large bowl of ice water. Let stand for 10 minutes. Drain. Transfer to very large bowl.

Add couscous and next 4 ingredients. Toss.

Lemon Mustard Dressing: Combine all 7 ingredients in jar with tight-fitting lid. Shake well. Makes about 1 cup (250 mL) dressing. Drizzle over couscous mixture. Toss. Makes about 10 cups (2.5 L).

1 cup (250 mL): 251 Calories; 4 g Total Fat (2.3 g Mono, 0.7 g Poly, 0.6 g Sat); trace Cholesterol; 46 g Carbohydrate; 5 g Fibre; 8 g Protein; 63 mg Sodium

Pictured on page 54.

Fresh Herb Dressing

An appetizing, tomato-based dressing with fresh garden herbs and a lingering spicy kick.

Low-sodium tomato juice	3/4 cup	175 mL
Pectin crystals (see Note)	1 tbsp.	15 mL
Lemon juice	1 tbsp.	15 mL
Garlic clove, minced (or 1/4 tsp., 1 mL, powder)	1	1
Finely chopped fresh sweet basil	1 tbsp.	15 mL
Finely chopped fresh parsley	1 tbsp.	15 mL
Pepper	1/4 tsp.	1 mL
Dried crushed chilies	1/8 tsp.	0.5 mL

Measure all 8 ingredients into jar with tight-fitting lid. Shake vigorously for 1 minute. Chill for about 15 minutes to blend flavours and until thickened. Makes about 1 cup (250 mL).

2 tbsp. (30 mL): 17 Calories; trace Total Fat (0 g Mono, 0 g Poly, 0 g Sat); 0 mg Cholesterol; 4 g Carbohydrate; trace Fibre; trace Protein; 54 mg Sodium

Note: The addition of pectin crystals to a vinegar-based dressing achieves about the same viscosity as if oil had been added.

Greens And Fruit Salad

A colourful and tantalizing mix of salad greens, fruit, toasted walnuts and red onion in a sweet, citrus dressing.

LEMON FLAXSEED DRESSING		
Frozen concentrated lemonade, thawed	2 tbsp.	30 mL
Liquid honey	2 tbsp.	30 mL
Flaxseed	1 tsp.	5 mL
Low-fat plain yogurt	6 tbsp.	100 mL
Mixed salad greens, loosely packed (about 7 oz., 200 g)	8 cups	2 L
Small cooking apple (such as McIntosh), with peel, cored and cut into thin wedges	1	1
Small navel orange, peeled, halved and thinly sliced	1	1
Seedless red grapes, halved	1 cup	250 mL
Very thinly sliced red onion	1/3 cup	75 mL
Walnuts, toasted (see Tip, page 29)	1/2 cup	125 mL

(continued on next page)

Lemon Flaxseed Dressing: Process first 4 ingredients in blender until flaxseed is broken up. Makes about 2/3 cup (150 mL) dressing.

Combine remaining 6 ingredients in large bowl. Drizzle dressing over top. Toss. Makes 8 cups (2 L).

1 cup (250 mL): 119 Calories; 4.8 g Total Fat (0.6 g Mono, 3.2 g Poly, 0.5 g Sat); trace Cholesterol; 18 g Carbohydrate; 3 g Fibre; 3 g Protein; 25 mg Sodium

Pictured on page 35.

Tangy Coleslaw

A finely textured coleslaw with a vibrant, honey mustard dressing. This will be a hit at your summer barbecue!

Finely shredded red cabbage	**6 cups**	**1.5 L**
Green onions, chopped	**12**	**12**
Celery ribs, thinly sliced	**3**	**3**
Medium oranges, peeled and chopped	**2**	**2**
ORANGE POPPY SEED DRESSING		
Freshly squeezed orange juice (about 1 small orange)	**1/4 cup**	**60 mL**
Liquid honey	**2 tbsp.**	**30 mL**
Dijon mustard	**2 tbsp.**	**30 mL**
Olive (or canola) oil	**1 tbsp.**	**15 mL**
Poppy seeds	**1 tbsp.**	**15 mL**
Pepper	**1/4 tsp.**	**1 mL**

Combine first 4 ingredients in large bowl.

Orange Poppy Seed Dressing: Combine all 6 ingredients in jar with tight-fitting lid. Shake well. Makes about 2/3 cup (150 mL) dressing. Drizzle over cabbage mixture. Toss. Makes about 10 cups (2.5 L).

1 cup (250 mL): 70 Calories; 2.2 g Total Fat (1.1 g Mono, 0.3 g Poly, 0.2 g Sat); 0 mg Cholesterol; 13 g Carbohydrate; 2 g Fibre; 2 g Protein; 93 mg Sodium

Caesar-Style Salad

A full-flavoured Caesar salad without the heaviness of a high-fat dressing.

Whole grain bread slices, crusts removed, cubed	4	4
Large head of romaine lettuce, torn	1	1
Shaved fresh Parmesan cheese (see Note)	1/4 cup	60 mL
CAESAR DRESSING		
Freshly squeezed lemon juice (about 1 medium lemon)	1/3 cup	75 mL
Finely grated fresh Parmesan cheese	2 tbsp.	30 mL
Anchovies (or 1 tbsp., 15 mL, paste)	2	2
Olive (or canola) oil	1 tbsp.	15 mL
Garlic clove, minced (or 1/4 tsp., 1 mL, powder)	1	1
Pepper	1/4 tsp.	1 mL

Arrange bread cubes on lightly greased baking sheet. Spray with cooking spray. Bake in 350°F (175°C) oven for about 15 minutes, stirring occasionally, until lightly browned. Cool completely.

Combine lettuce and shaved Parmesan cheese in large bowl.

Caesar Dressing: Process all 6 ingredients in blender until smooth. Makes about 1/2 cup (125 mL) dressing. Drizzle over lettuce mixture. Add bread cubes. Toss. Makes 10 cups (2.5 L).

1 cup (250 mL): 62 Calories; 3.2 g Total Fat (1.7 g Mono, 0.4 g Poly, 1 g Sat); 4 mg Cholesterol; 6 g Carbohydrate; 1 g Fibre; 3 g Protein; 114 mg Sodium

Note: Use Parmesan cheese shaver or vegetable peeler to shave thin slices from block of Parmesan cheese.

Reduce fat in your diet by using less dressing or a low-fat dressing on your salad. Measure your salad dressing rather than just pouring straight from the bottle or cruet onto your salad.

Mulligatawny Soup

Muhl-ih-guh-TAW-nee, which means "pepper water," is a traditional soup from India. A creamy, warmly spiced soup of potatoes, apples, lentils and onions. Serve with a dollop of low-fat yogurt and fresh cilantro.

Chopped onion	1 1/2 cups	375 mL
Garlic cloves, minced (or 1/2 tsp., 2 mL, powder)	2	2
Finely grated gingerroot (or 1/2 tsp., 2 mL, ground ginger)	2 tsp.	10 mL
Fresh small chilies, chopped	2	2
Curry powder	1 tbsp.	15 mL
Ground cumin	1/4 – 2 tsp.	1 – 10 mL
Ground coriander	1/4 – 2 tsp.	1 – 10 mL
Canola oil	2 tsp.	10 mL
Cinnamon stick (4 inch, 10 cm, length)	1	1
Whole green cardamom, bruised (see Tip, page 103)	6 – 8	6 – 8
Red lentils	1 1/4 cups	300 mL
Chicken Stock, page 12 (or Vegetable Stock, page 14)	8 cups	2 L
Medium potatoes, peeled and chopped	2	2
Medium cooking apples (such as McIntosh), peeled, cored and chopped	2	2
Buttermilk (or reconstituted from powder)	1 1/2 cups	375 mL
Fresh cilantro (or parsley) leaves	3 tbsp.	50 mL

Sauté first 7 ingredients in canola oil in large pot or Dutch oven for about 5 minutes until onion is soft.

Add next 6 ingredients. Stir. Bring to a boil. Reduce heat to medium-low. Cover. Simmer for about 25 minutes, stirring occasionally, until lentils and potato are soft. Cool slightly. Remove and discard cinnamon stick and cardamom. Process in blender, in 2 to 3 batches, until smooth. Return to pot.

Add buttermilk and cilantro. Heat and stir on medium for 5 to 7 minutes until heated through. Makes about 12 cups (3 L).

1 cup (250 mL): 169 Calories; 2.7 g Total Fat (0.9 g Mono, 0.5 g Poly, 0.7 g Sat); 4 mg Cholesterol; 27 g Carbohydrate; 5 g Fibre; 10 g Protein; 63 mg Sodium

Full O' Beans Soup

A robust mixed bean soup with a colourful tomato-flavoured broth. A hearty and satisfying dish.

Mixed dried beans (such as chickpeas, yellow split peas, green, lima, pinto or red kidney beans), see Note	**1 1/2 cups**	**375 mL**
Chicken Stock, page 12	**6 cups**	**1.5 L**
Water	**2 1/2 cups**	**625 mL**
Large onion, chopped	**1**	**1**
Garlic cloves, minced (or 1/4 – 1/2 tsp., 1 – 2 mL, powder)	**1 – 2**	**1 – 2**
Olive (or canola) oil	**1 tbsp.**	**15 mL**
Roasted Tomato Sauce, page 135	**1 cup**	**250 mL**
Chopped celery	**1/2 cup**	**125 mL**
Medium carrot, thinly sliced	**1**	**1**
Granulated sugar	**1 tsp.**	**5 mL**
Ground marjoram	**1/4 tsp.**	**1 mL**
Dried sweet basil	**1/4 tsp.**	**1 mL**
Pepper	**1/4 tsp.**	**1 mL**

Combine beans, stock and water in large pot or Dutch oven. Bring to a boil. Reduce heat to medium-low. Cover. Simmer for about 2 hours, without stirring, until beans are tender.

Cook onion and garlic in olive oil in large non-stick frying pan on medium for about 10 minutes, stirring occasionally, until onion is soft and starting to caramelize. Add to beans.

Add remaining 7 ingredients. Bring to a boil. Reduce heat. Cover. Simmer for about 45 minutes, stirring occasionally, until vegetables are tender-crisp. Makes 8 cups (2 L).

1 cup (250 mL): 188 Calories; 4 g Total Fat (1.9 g Mono, 0.8 g Poly, 0.8 g Sat); 2 mg Cholesterol; 28 g Carbohydrate; 8 g Fibre; 11 g Protein; 85 mg Sodium

Note: Make your own bean mixture or mixed beans may be purchased in the bulk section of the grocery store or in prepackaged bags.

Chicken Tomato Soup

A spicy, tomato-based soup with tender pieces of chicken, hearty chickpeas and fresh garden mint.

Boneless, skinless chicken breast halves (about 4)	**1 lb.**	**454 g**
Chopped onion	**1 cup**	**250 mL**
Garlic cloves, minced (or 3/4 tsp., 4 mL, powder)	**3**	**3**
Chili paste (sambal oelek)	**1 tsp.**	**5 mL**
Canola oil	**2 tsp.**	**10 mL**
Chicken Stock, page 12	**4 cups**	**1 L**
Roasted Tomato Sauce, page 135	**2 cups**	**500 mL**
Chickpeas, page 15	**1 cup**	**250 mL**
Chopped fresh mint leaves (or 3/4 – 3 3/4 tsp., 4 – 19 mL, dried)	**1 – 5 tbsp.**	**15 – 75 mL**
Crumbled feta cheese (optional)		
Chopped fresh mint leaves (optional)		

Cook chicken on greased electric grill over medium heat for about 5 minutes per side until no longer pink inside. Cut crosswise into 1/4 inch (6 mm) strips about 2 inches (5 cm) long. Set aside.

Sauté onion, garlic and chili paste in canola oil in large pot or Dutch oven for about 5 minutes until onion is soft.

Add chicken and next 4 ingredients. Heat and stir on medium until mixture is heated through.

Sprinkle individual servings with feta cheese and mint. Makes 8 cups (2 L).

1 cup (250 mL): 155 Calories; 4.2 g Total Fat (1.5 g Mono, 1.1 g Poly, 0.8 g Sat); 35 mg Cholesterol; 12 g Carbohydrate; 3 g Fibre; 17 g Protein; 78 mg Sodium

Pictured on page 71.

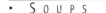

Creamy Yam Soup

A thick, sweet soup perfect for those cold winter evenings. Garnish with a dollop of low-fat sour cream and chopped chives. Serve with warm crusty whole wheat rolls.

Chopped onion	1 1/2 cups	375 mL
Garlic cloves, minced (or 1/2 – 1 tsp., 2 – 5 mL, powder)	2 – 4	2 – 4
Ground ginger	1 tsp.	5 mL
Pepper	1/4 tsp.	1 mL
Canola oil	2 tsp.	10 mL
Chicken Stock, page 12	6 – 7 cups	1.5 – 1.75 L
Small yams (or sweet potatoes), about 1 lb. (454 g), chopped	2	2
Dried sweet basil	1 tsp.	5 mL
Buttermilk (or reconstituted from powder)	1 cup	250 mL

Sauté first 4 ingredients in canola oil in large pot or Dutch oven for about 5 minutes until onion is soft.

Add stock, yam and basil. Stir. Bring to a boil. Reduce heat to medium. Cover. Simmer for about 20 minutes, stirring occasionally, until yam is tender. Cool slightly. Process in blender, in 2 to 3 batches, until smooth. Return to pot.

Add buttermilk. Heat and stir on medium for about 5 minutes until heated through. Makes about 10 cups (2.5 L).

1 cup (250 mL): 146 Calories; 2.9 g Total Fat (1 g Mono, 0.6 g Poly, 0.7 g Sat); 3 mg Cholesterol; 25 g Carbohydrate; 4 g Fibre; 6 g Protein; 68 mg Sodium

1. Pumpkin And Herb Biscuits, page 43
2. Cream Of Asparagus Soup, page 75
3. Chicken Tomato Soup, page 69

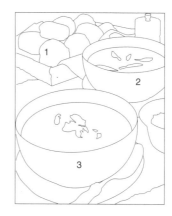

Cheesy Broccoli Soup

This thick, cheesy soup is best served with warm crusty rolls and a crisp green salad. A warm and welcoming comfort food on a cold winter day.

Chicken Stock, page 12	**3 cups**	**750 mL**
Finely chopped onion	**2/3 cup**	**150 mL**
Box of frozen chopped broccoli, thawed and finely chopped	**10 oz.**	**300 g**
Can of skim evaporated milk	**13 1/2 oz.**	**385 mL**
Pepper	**1/8 tsp.**	**0.5 mL**
Skim milk	**1/3 cup**	**75 mL**
All-purpose flour	**2 tbsp.**	**30 mL**
Grated low-fat sharp Cheddar cheese	**1 cup**	**250 mL**

Bring stock and onion to a boil in large saucepan. Reduce heat to medium. Cover. Simmer for about 5 minutes until onion is partially softened.

Add broccoli, evaporated milk and pepper. Heat and stir for about 5 minutes until boiling and thickened.

Stir skim milk into flour in small bowl until smooth. Stir into soup. Heat and stir for about 5 minutes until boiling and thickened.

Add cheese. Heat and stir until cheese is melted. Makes about 6 cups (1.5 L).

1 cup (250 mL): 139 Calories; 2.7 g Total Fat (0.8 g Mono, trace Poly, 1.3 g Sat); 8 mg Cholesterol; 15 g Carbohydrate; 2 g Fibre; 14 g Protein; 235 mg Sodium

1. Lebanese Fattoush Salad, page 62
2. Spiced Iced Tea, page 30
3. Potato Pepper Salad, page 59
4. Beef And Eggplant Burgers, page 78

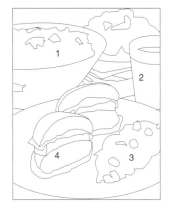

Spinach And Meatball Soup

Flavourful meatballs are cooked in a beefy broth of tomatoes, carrots and pasta. Fresh spinach and basil add an attractive splash of colour.

MEATBALLS

Grated light Parmesan cheese	2 tbsp.	30 mL
Fine dry bread crumbs	1/4 cup	60 mL
Milk	2 tbsp.	30 mL
Garlic cloves, minced (or 1/4 – 1/2 tsp., 1 – 2 mL, powder)	1 – 2	1 – 2
Parsley flakes	2 tsp.	10 mL
Pepper	1/8 tsp.	0.5 mL
Lean ground pork	6 oz.	170 g
Extra lean ground beef	6 oz.	170 g

SOUP

Beef Stock, page 13	8 cups	2 L
Stewed Tomatoes, with juice, page 20	2 cups	500 mL
Grated carrot	1/2 cup	125 mL
Dried sweet basil	1/2 tsp.	2 mL
Anellini ring pasta (or other tiny pasta)	1 cup	250 mL
Fresh spinach leaves, stems removed, packed and sliced (or 10 oz., 300 g, box of frozen chopped spinach, thawed and squeezed dry)	2 1/2 cups	625 mL

Meatballs: Combine first 6 ingredients in medium bowl. Add ground pork and ground beef. Mix well. Shape into balls, using 1 tsp. (5 mL) for each (see Tip, page 75). Makes 64 meatballs.

Soup: Combine stock, tomatoes with juice, carrot and basil in large pot or Dutch oven. Bring to a boil. Reduce heat to maintain gentle boil.

Add meatballs and pasta. Cover. Simmer for about 5 minutes until meatballs are no longer pink in centre and pasta is al dente.

Add spinach. Stir. Simmer, uncovered, for 2 to 3 minutes until spinach is wilted and pasta is tender. Makes 12 cups (3 L).

1 cup (250 mL): 143 Calories; 4.5 g Total Fat (1.5 g Mono, 0.6 g Poly, 1.4 g Sat); 15 mg Cholesterol; 16 g Carbohydrate; 2 g Fibre; 11 g Protein; 147 mg Sodium

Cream Of Asparagus Soup

A creamy , aromatic soup with the mild and delectable taste of asparagus. Make a large batch when asparagus is in season and freeze. Serve with warm crusty rolls.

Chicken Stock, page 12	1/4 cup	60 mL
Chopped onion	3/4 cup	175 mL
All-purpose flour	2 tbsp.	30 mL
Milk	2 cups	500 mL
Chicken Stock, page 12	1 1/2 cups	375 mL
Fresh asparagus spears, trimmed of tough ends and chopped	1 lb.	454 g
Lemon juice	1 tbsp.	15 mL
Coarsely ground pepper	1/2 tsp.	2 mL

Heat first amount of stock in large pot or Dutch oven on medium. Add onion. Cook for about 10 minutes until onion is soft.

Add flour. Heat and stir for about 1 minute to cook flour. Gradually stir in milk until well combined. Add second amount of stock. Heat and stir for about 5 minutes until boiling and thickened.

Add asparagus. Stir. Cook for 5 to 10 minutes, stirring occasionally, until asparagus is tender. Cool slightly. Process in blender, in 2 batches, until smooth. Return to pot.

Add lemon juice and pepper. Heat and stir on medium for about 2 minutes until heated through. Makes about 4 cups (1 L).

1 cup (250 mL): 111 Calories; 2.3 g Total Fat (0.5 g Mono, 0.3 g Poly, 1.1 g Sat); 9 mg Cholesterol; 15 g Carbohydrate; 1 g Fibre; 9 g Protein; 88 mg Sodium

Pictured on page 71.

To make uniform-size meatballs, pack meat mixture evenly into plastic wrap-lined 8 x 8 inch (20 x 20 cm) pan. Lift out of pan using plastic wrap and place on work surface. Cut 8 rows each way with a blunt-edged tool, such as a pancake lifter or the dull side of a knife. Roll or shape each piece into a ball.

Beef And Lentil Chili

Serve over toasted hamburger buns for fun and tasty sloppy joes or enjoy as is with fresh bread or biscuits. A spicy chili that calls for several of our "basics" recipes. Use less chili powder if desired.

Extra lean ground beef	**1 lb.**	**454 g**
Chopped onion	**1 1/2 cups**	**375 mL**
Chopped celery	**1 1/2 cups**	**375 mL**
Chopped green or yellow pepper	**1 cup**	**250 mL**
Beef Stock, page 13	**1 cup**	**250 mL**
Garlic cloves, minced (or 1/2 – 1 tsp., 2 – 5 mL, powder)	**2 – 4**	**2 – 4**
Good-For-All Ketchup, page 131	**2 cups**	**500 mL**
Green Lentils, page 16	**2 cups**	**500 mL**
Roasted Tomato Sauce, page 135	**1 cup**	**250 mL**
Cans of red kidney beans (14 oz., 398 mL, each), drained and rinsed	**2**	**2**
Chili powder	**1 tbsp.**	**15 mL**
Ground cumin	**1/4 – 1 tsp.**	**1 – 5 mL**
Dried oregano	**1/2 – 1 tsp.**	**2 – 5 mL**
Dried crushed chilies	**1/4 tsp.**	**1 mL**
Pepper, sprinkle		

Scramble-fry ground beef in large non-stick frying pan on medium-high until no longer pink. Drain. Turn into large pot or Dutch oven.

Add next 5 ingredients. Cook, uncovered, on medium for 15 to 20 minutes, stirring occasionally, until onion is soft and most of stock is absorbed.

Add remaining 9 ingredients. Bring to a boil, stirring frequently to prevent burning. Reduce heat to medium-low. Cover. Simmer for 20 to 30 minutes, stirring occasionally, until slightly thickened to desired consistency. Makes 9 cups (2.25 L). Serves 6.

1 serving: 391 Calories; 3.9 g Total Fat (1.2 g Mono, 0.4 g Poly, 1.1 g Sat); 19 mg Cholesterol; 64 g Carbohydrate; 20 g Fibre; 27 g Protein; 298 mg Sodium

Steak With Spice Coating

The taste of these juicy, grilled steaks is complemented by a delicious sesame seed and curry coating. Top with this uniquely flavoured salsa for a sensational dinner treat.

Sesame seeds	2 tbsp.	30 mL
Curry powder	1 tbsp.	15 mL
Coarsely ground pepper	2 tsp.	10 mL
Beef tenderloin steaks (about 4 oz., 113 g, each), cut about 1 inch (2.5 cm) thick	4	4
PAPAYA COCONUT SALSA		
Chopped ripe papaya	1 cup	250 mL
Flake coconut, toasted (see Tip, page 29)	1/4 cup	60 mL
Chopped fresh mint leaves (or 3/4 – 1 1/2 tsp., 4 – 7 mL, dried)	1 – 2 tbsp.	15 – 30 mL
Sweet (or regular) chili sauce	2 tbsp.	30 mL
White wine vinegar	1 tbsp.	15 mL

Combine sesame seeds, curry powder and pepper in shallow dish.

Roll edge of each steak in sesame seed mixture to coat. Cook on greased electric grill over medium heat for 5 to 7 minutes per side until desired doneness.

Papaya Coconut Salsa: Combine all 5 ingredients in small bowl. Makes 1 1/4 cups (300 mL) salsa. Serve with steaks. Serves 4.

1 serving: 267 Calories; 13.8 g Total Fat (4.1 g Mono, 1.3 g Poly, 6.3 g Sat); 70 mg Cholesterol; 10 g Carbohydrate; 3 g Fibre; 25 g Protein; 302 mg Sodium

Pictured on page 108.

A simple way to reduce fat in your diet is to reduce serving sizes. A commonly recommended serving for meat is the size of a deck of cards (about 4 oz., 113 g, uncooked).

Beef And Eggplant Burgers

These fancy, gourmet burgers are low in fat. The balsamic vinegar gives the mild eggplant a little zest, while the Cheddar cheese adds a rich edge to the overall flavour.

Black Beans, page 14	1 1/2 cups	375 mL
Extra lean ground beef	3/4 lb.	340 g
Whole wheat bread crumbs	1/3 cup	75 mL
Finely chopped red onion	1/2 cup	125 mL
Grated light sharp Cheddar cheese	1/3 cup	75 mL
Garlic cloves, minced (or 1/2 tsp., 2 mL, powder)	2	2
Ground cumin	1 tsp.	5 mL
Hot pepper sauce	1/2 – 1 tsp.	2 – 5 mL
Pepper	1/2 tsp.	2 mL
Small eggplant, cut into 1/4 inch (6 mm) thick slices	1	1
Balsamic vinegar	1 – 2 tbsp.	15 – 30 mL
Whole wheat hamburger buns, split and toasted	6	6
Red Pepper Sauce, page 134	1/2 cup	125 mL
Arugula (or spinach) leaves, trimmed, packed	1 cup	250 mL

Process first 4 ingredients in food processor until well combined. Transfer to large bowl.

Add next 5 ingredients. Mix well. Shape into 6 patties, using 1/2 cup (125 mL) for each. Cook on greased electric grill over medium heat for about 8 minutes per side until no longer pink inside.

Spray eggplant with cooking spray. Cook on greased grill for 2 to 3 minutes per side until golden brown. Drizzle with vinegar.

Spread cut sides of buns with Red Pepper Sauce. Place 1 patty on bottom half of each bun. Divide and layer with eggplant and arugula. Cover with top half of each bun. Makes 6 burgers.

1 burger: 343 Calories; 9.6 g Total Fat (4.1 g Mono, 1.2 g Poly, 3.1 g Sat); 22 mg Cholesterol; 42 g Carbohydrate; 8 g Fibre; 23 g Protein; 333 mg Sodium

Pictured on page 72.

Beef And Corn Bake

This easy-to-make dish combines the taste of scrambled beef with taco seasoning and sweet nuggets of corn. Serve with your favourite salsa and some low-fat sour cream. This is a dish the kids will love!

Extra lean ground beef	**1 lb.**	**454 g**
Large egg	**1**	**1**
Skim evaporated milk	**2/3 cup**	**150 mL**
Chopped onion	**1 cup**	**250 mL**
Envelope of 25% less salt taco seasoning mix	**1 1/4 oz.**	**35 g**
Pepper	**1/4 tsp.**	**1 mL**
Fresh bread crumbs	**1 cup**	**250 mL**
Frozen kernel corn	**2 cups**	**500 mL**
Chopped fresh chives	**1 tbsp.**	**15 mL**

Scramble-fry ground beef in large non-stick frying pan on medium-high for about 10 minutes until browned. Drain well.

Beat egg with fork in large bowl. Add next 5 ingredients. Mix well.

Add corn, chives and beef. Mix well. Press into greased 9 x 9 inch (22 x 22 cm) pan. Bake in 350°F (175°C) oven for about 40 minutes until browned and set. Serves 6.

1 serving: 318 Calories; 9.6 g Total Fat (3.9 g Mono, 0.8 g Poly, 3.3 g Sat); 64 mg Cholesterol; 35 g Carbohydrate; 2 g Fibre; 24 g Protein; 458 mg Sodium

TURKEY AND CORN BAKE: Omit ground beef. Use extra lean ground turkey.

To make a smaller serving of meat appear larger, place uncooked meat between 2 layers of plastic wrap and pound with a mallet, rolling pin or edge of a small plate until thin.

Veal And Asparagus Rolls

The moist, tender veal looks very appealing wrapped around crisp asparagus spears. The hint of wine, basil and Parmesan cheese is delightful.

Fresh asparagus spears, trimmed of tough ends	1/2 lb.	225 g
Water		
Ice water		
Veal scallopini (about 1 lb., 454 g)	8	8
Grainy mustard	1 1/2 tbsp.	25 mL
Finely grated fresh Parmesan cheese	2 tbsp.	30 mL
Pepper, sprinkle		
Dry white (or alcohol-free) wine	1/2 cup	125 mL
Chopped fresh sweet basil (or 3/4 – 3 tsp., 4 – 15 mL, dried)	1 – 4 tbsp.	15 – 60 mL
Liquid honey	2 tbsp.	30 mL
Chopped fresh small chilies	2 tsp.	10 mL
Olive (or canola) oil	1 tsp.	5 mL
Garlic cloves, minced (or 1/2 tsp., 2 mL, powder)	2	2
Red Pepper Sauce, page 134	1 cup	250 mL

Cook asparagus in water in large frying pan on high for 2 to 3 minutes until bright green.

Plunge asparagus into ice water in medium bowl. Let stand for 5 to 10 minutes until cool. Drain.

Lay scallopini on work surface. Gently pound with meat mallet or rolling pin until 1/8 inch (3 mm) thick. Spread 1 side with 1/8 of mustard. Lay 2 asparagus spears down centre of each scallopini over mustard. Sprinkle with 1/8 of Parmesan cheese and sprinkle of pepper. Roll up. Secure with wooden picks. Repeat with remaining scallopini, mustard, asparagus, Parmesan cheese and pepper.

Combine next 6 ingredients in large bowl. Add veal rolls. Turn gently to coat completely. Cover. Chill for at least 8 hours or overnight. Cook on greased electric grill over medium heat for about 10 minutes, turning occasionally, until tender and desired doneness. Makes 8 veal rolls.

Heat and stir sauce in small saucepan on medium until hot. Divide and spoon about 1/4 cup (60 mL) sauce onto 4 individual plates. Lay 2 veal rolls on top of sauce. Serves 4.

1 serving: 239 Calories; 4.4 g Total Fat (1.8 g Mono, 0.4 g Poly, 1.4 g Sat); 91 mg Cholesterol; 17 g Carbohydrate; 3 g Fibre; 28 g Protein; 240 mg Sodium

Philippines Stew

This is a spicy stew of sausage, chicken, sweet potato and rice. The bananas add a unique and distinctly tropical flavour.

Sausage meat	**1/2 lb.**	**225 g**
Chopped onion	**1 1/2 cups**	**375 mL**
Garlic cloves, minced (or 3/4 – 1 1/4 tsp., 4 – 6 mL, powder)	**3 – 5**	**3 – 5**
Finely chopped gingerroot (or 1/2 tsp., 2 mL, ground ginger)	**2 tsp.**	**10 mL**
Cayenne pepper	**1/4 tsp.**	**1 mL**
Chicken Stock, page 12	**3 cups**	**750 mL**
Stewed Tomatoes, with juice, page 20	**2 cups**	**500 mL**
Bay leaf	**1**	**1**
Boneless, skinless chicken breast halves (about 4), cut into 1 1/2 inch (3.8 cm) chunks	**1 lb.**	**454 g**
Chickpeas, page 15	**1 1/2 cups**	**375 mL**
Cubed sweet potato (or yam), about 1 lb. (454 g)	**3 cups**	**750 mL**
Brown converted rice, uncooked	**1 cup**	**250 mL**
Sliced baby bok choy (about 2 medium)	**4 cups**	**1 L**
Underripe bananas, sliced 1/2 inch (12 mm) thick	**2**	**2**
Green onions, thinly sliced	**4**	**4**

Scramble-fry sausage meat in large uncovered pot or Dutch oven until browned. Drain. Rinse with warm water. Drain. Return to pot.

Add onion, garlic and ginger. Heat and stir on medium-high for about 5 minutes until onion is soft. Sprinkle with cayenne pepper. Stir.

Add next 7 ingredients. Bring to a boil. Reduce heat to medium-low. Cover. Simmer for about 40 minutes, stirring once or twice, until rice is tender. Remove and discard bay leaf.

Stir in bok choy, banana and green onion. Cover. Cook for 5 to 10 minutes until heated through. Makes 12 cups (3 L). Serves 6.

1 serving: 511 Calories; 9.6 g Total Fat (3.2 g Mono, 2.2 g Poly, 2.4 g Sat); 62 mg Cholesterol; 76 g Carbohydrate; 12 g Fibre; 31 g Protein; 285 mg Sodium

Cacciatore Casserole

Peppery, tender chicken slices rest in a thick tomato sauce flavoured with wine, garlic and mushrooms. This is a dense casserole, topped with a layer of melted cheese. Assemble ahead of time and chill until needed.

Garlic cloves, minced (or 1/4 – 1/2 tsp., 1 – 2 mL, powder)	1 – 2	1 – 2
Diced green pepper	1/2 cup	125 mL
Small onion, diced	1	1
Sliced fresh mushrooms	1 cup	250 mL
Olive (or canola) oil	1 tsp.	5 mL
Boneless, skinless chicken breast halves (about 2), thinly sliced	1/2 lb.	225 g
Pepper	1/8 tsp.	0.5 mL
Olive (or canola) oil	1 tsp.	5 mL
Chicken Stock, page 12	1 cup	250 mL
Stewed Tomatoes, with juice, page 20, mashed	1 cup	250 mL
Dry red (or alcohol-free) wine	1/4 cup	60 mL
Can of tomato paste	5 1/2 oz.	156 mL
Granulated sugar	1 tsp.	5 mL
Dried sweet basil	1 tsp.	5 mL
Dried oregano	1 tsp.	5 mL
Bay leaf	1	1
Large yolk-free broad egg noodles (about 8 oz., 225 g)	5 cups	1.25 L
Boiling water	8 cups	2 L
Grated part-skim mozzarella cheese	3/4 cup	175 mL
Grated light Parmesan cheese	2 tbsp.	30 mL

Sauté garlic, green pepper, onion and mushrooms in first amount of olive oil in large non-stick frying pan for about 4 minutes until onion is soft. Remove to small bowl.

Sauté chicken, sprinkled with pepper, in second amount of olive oil in same frying pan until no longer pink. Add to mushroom mixture.

Put stock, tomato with juice, wine and tomato paste into same frying pan. Stir until smooth.

Add sugar, basil, oregano and bay leaf. Stir. Bring to a boil. Add chicken mixture. Simmer, uncovered, on medium-low for about 15 minutes until slightly reduced and thickened. Remove and discard bay leaf.

(continued on next page)

Cook noodles in boiling water in large uncovered pot or Dutch oven for about 5 minutes, stirring occasionally, until tender but firm. Drain. Add to sauce. Stir. Pour into greased 2 quart (2 L) casserole.

Sprinkle with mozzarella cheese and Parmesan cheese. Cover. Bake in 350°F (175°C) oven for 25 to 30 minutes until bubbly and heated through. Serves 4.

1 serving: 482 Calories; 10 g Total Fat (3.7 g Mono, 1.3 g Poly, 3.9 g Sat); 48 mg Cholesterol; 65 g Carbohydrate; 6 g Fibre; 34 g Protein; 377 mg Sodium

Chicken Meatballs

These spicy chicken balls are flavoured with fresh herbs and baked in a zesty tomato sauce.

Lean ground chicken	1 lb.	454 g
Chopped fresh oregano leaves (or 3/4 – 2 1/4 tsp., 4 – 11 mL, dried)	1 – 3 tbsp.	15 – 50 mL
Chopped fresh sweet basil (or 3/4 – 2 1/4 tsp., 4 – 11 mL, dried)	1 – 3 tbsp.	15 – 50 mL
Large egg, fork-beaten	1	1
Fresh whole wheat bread crumbs	2/3 cup	150 mL
Garlic cloves, minced (or 1/2 tsp., 2 mL, powder)	2	2
Chili paste (sambal oelek)	1/2 – 1 tsp.	2 – 5 mL
Pepper	1/4 – 1/2 tsp.	1 – 2 mL
Ground cinnamon	1/4 – 1/2 tsp.	1 – 2 mL
Roasted Tomato Sauce, page 135	1 cup	250 mL
Chicken Stock, page 12	1/2 cup	125 mL

Put first 9 ingredients into large bowl. Mix well. Cover. Chill for 1 hour. Shape into balls, using 2 tbsp. (30 mL) mixture for each. Arrange on greased baking sheets. Bake in 375°F (190°C) oven 10 to 15 minutes until lightly browned. Transfer to ungreased 2 quart (2 L) casserole.

Combine sauce and stock in small bowl. Pour evenly over meatballs. Bake, uncovered, for about 25 minutes until sauce is heated through. Serves 4.

1 serving: 243 Calories; 4.2 g Total Fat (1.3 g Mono, 0.8 g Poly, 1.1 g Sat); 119 mg Cholesterol; 18 g Carbohydrate; 1 g Fibre; 31 g Protein; 312 mg Sodium

Pictured on page 125.

Chicken Asparagus Pasta

The grilled flavour of the chicken, red peppers and asparagus is enhanced by a lemon and honey dressing. Combine this with whole wheat spaghettini and you have one sensational dish.

Boneless, skinless chicken breast halves (about 4)	1 lb.	454 g
Small red peppers, quartered	2	2
Fresh asparagus spears, trimmed of tough ends	1/2 lb.	225 g
Whole wheat spaghettini	9 oz.	255 g
Boiling water	8 cups	2 L
Chopped fresh parsley (or 1 – 2 tbsp., 15 – 30 mL, flakes)	1/4 – 1/2 cup	60 – 125 mL
Freshly squeezed lemon juice (about 1 small lemon)	1/4 cup	60 mL
Liquid honey	3 tbsp.	50 mL
Grainy mustard	1 1/2 tbsp.	25 mL
Olive (or canola) oil	2 tsp.	10 mL
Finely shaved fresh Parmesan cheese, sprinkle		

Cook chicken on greased electric grill over medium heat for about 5 minutes per side until no longer pink inside. Cut into 1/4 inch (6 mm) thick slices. Cover. Keep warm.

Spray red pepper and asparagus with cooking spray. Cook on greased grill over medium heat for 5 to 7 minutes, turning occasionally, until tender-crisp. Cut pepper into 1/2 inch (12 mm) thick strips. Cut each asparagus spear in half. Cover. Keep warm.

Cook spaghettini in boiling water in large uncovered pot or Dutch oven for 8 to 10 minutes, stirring occasionally, until tender but firm. Drain well. Return to same pot. Add chicken, red pepper and asparagus. Toss.

Combine next 5 ingredients in jar with tight-fitting lid. Shake well. Drizzle over spaghettini mixture. Toss to coat.

Sprinkle individual servings with Parmesan cheese. Makes 8 cups (2 L). Serves 4.

1 serving: 427 Calories; 6.5 g Total Fat (3 g Mono, 1.3 g Poly, 1.3 g Sat); 63 mg Cholesterol; 63 g Carbohydrate; 9 g Fibre; 33 g Protein; 167 mg Sodium

Chicken Spinach Strudel

Crispy, golden pastry wrapped around a mild, creamy filling of chicken and spinach. The raisins and pine nuts are a nice addition.

Box of frozen chopped spinach, thawed and squeezed dry	10 oz.	300 g
Chopped cooked chicken (breast is best)	3 cups	750 mL
Block of light cream cheese, cut up and softened	4 oz.	125 g
Dark raisins, finely chopped	1/3 cup	75 mL
Honey mustard	3 tbsp.	50 mL
Large egg, fork-beaten	1	1
Pepper	1/2 tsp.	2 mL
Pine nuts (optional), toasted (see Tip, page 29)	1/4 cup	60 mL
Frozen phyllo pastry sheets, thawed according to package directions	6	6

Combine first 8 ingredients in large bowl until cream cheese is well mixed.

Lay tea towel, short end closest to you, on work surface. Place 1 pastry sheet on tea towel with short end of pastry closest to you. Place second pastry sheet above first pastry sheet on tea towel, overlapping 4 inches (10 cm) in middle. Cover remaining pastry sheets with slightly damp tea towel to prevent drying out. Working quickly, lightly spray pastry sheets (now 1 long sheet) with cooking spray. Place 2 more pastry sheets on top in same manner. Lightly spray with cooking spray. Repeat with remaining 2 pastry sheets. Lightly spray with cooking spray. Mound chicken mixture evenly across short end of pastry stack, 6 inches (15 cm) from bottom edge, to make log about 3 1/2 inches (9 cm) in diameter. Fold bottom edge of pastry up and over chicken mixture. Roll up tightly, using tea towel to assist. Pack any loose chicken mixture back into roll. Do not tuck in sides. Place, seam-side down, on greased baking sheet. Spray top and sides lightly with cooking spray. Bake in 425°F (220°C) oven for about 15 minutes until golden brown and heated through. Cuts into 8 slices.

1 slice: 229 Calories; 8.0 g Total Fat (2.8 g Mono, 1.5 g Poly, 2.9 g Sat); 80 mg Cholesterol; 18 g Carbohydrate; 2 g Fibre; 21 g Protein; 204 mg Sodium

Pictured on back cover.

Stuffed Chicken Breast

Dream of the Mediterranean while you enjoy the enticing flavours of red peppers, artichokes and sweet basil.

STUFFING

Medium leek (white and tender parts only), thinly sliced	1	1
Garlic cloves, minced (or 1/2 tsp., 2 mL, powder)	2	2
Finely chopped red pepper	1/2 cup	125 mL
Olive (or canola) oil	1 tsp.	5 mL
Jar of marinated artichokes, drained and chopped	6 oz.	170 g
Balsamic vinegar	1 tbsp.	15 mL
Brown sugar, packed	1 tbsp.	15 mL
Chopped fresh sweet basil (or 3/4 – 2 1/4 tsp., 4 – 11 mL, dried)	1 – 3 tbsp.	15 – 50 mL
Boneless, skinless chicken breast halves (about 2 lbs., 900 g)	8	8
All-purpose flour	1/2 cup	125 mL
Fine dry whole wheat bread crumbs	1 1/2 cups	375 mL
Large eggs	2	2
Milk	2 tbsp.	30 mL

Stuffing: Sauté leek, garlic and red pepper in olive oil in large non-stick frying pan for about 5 minutes until leek is soft. Reduce heat to medium.

Add artichoke, vinegar and brown sugar. Heat and stir until sugar is dissolved. Remove from heat.

Add basil. Stir. Makes about 1 1/4 cups (300 mL) stuffing.

Cut deep horizontal pocket into 1 side of each chicken breast almost through to other side. Fill each pocket with 2 1/2 tbsp. (37 mL) stuffing. Secure openings with wooden picks.

Put flour and bread crumbs into separate shallow dishes. Beat eggs and milk with fork in small bowl until well combined. Dredge chicken in flour to coat. Dip into egg mixture. Dip into bread crumbs to coat completely. Place on greased baking sheet. Spray chicken with cooking spray. Bake in 350°F (175°C) oven for about 25 minutes until chicken is golden and no longer pink inside. Cool slightly. Remove wooden picks. To serve, cut chicken in half diagonally. Serves 8.

1 serving: 295 Calories; 7.6 g Total Fat (2.4 g Mono, 1.3 g Poly, 1.5 g Sat); 115 mg Cholesterol; 28 g Carbohydrate; 2 g Fibre; 28 g Protein; 321 mg Sodium

Chicken Stew

A colourful stew, full of chicken and root vegetables and flavoured delicately with white wine. This makes a delicious, comforting meal.

All-purpose flour	**3 tbsp.**	**50 mL**
Bone-in, skinless chicken thighs, trimmed of fat (about 2 1/2 lbs., 1.1 kg)	**12**	**12**
Olive (or canola) oil	**2 tsp.**	**10 mL**
Large onion, halved and sliced	**1**	**1**
Small yellow turnip, cut into 1 inch (2.5 cm) cubes	**1**	**1**
Large carrots, cut into 1 inch (2.5 cm) cubes	**2**	**2**
Large potato, cut into 1 inch (2.5 cm) cubes	**1**	**1**
Chicken Stock, page 12	**1 cup**	**250 mL**
Dry white (or alcohol-free) wine	**1 cup**	**250 mL**
Pepper	**1/4 tsp.**	**1 mL**
Frozen (or fresh) peas	**1/2 cup**	**125 mL**

Measure flour into shallow dish. Dredge chicken in flour to coat well. Cook chicken, in 2 batches, in olive oil in large pot or Dutch oven on medium for about 3 minutes per side until browned.

Add next 7 ingredients. Stir. Bring to a boil. Reduce heat to low. Cover. Simmer for 20 minutes. Remove cover. Simmer for 30 minutes, stirring occasionally. Increase heat to medium-high. Boil for about 5 minutes until chicken is very tender and sauce is slightly thickened.

Add peas. Stir. Cook for about 3 minutes until peas are heated through. Makes about 9 cups (2.25 L). Serves 6.

1 serving: 268 Calories; 10.1 g Total Fat (4.3 g Mono, 2.1 g Poly, 2.6 g Sat); 75 mg Cholesterol; 19 g Carbohydrate; 3 g Fibre; 24 g Protein; 107 mg Sodium

Pictured on page 53.

Choose skinless chicken when preparing meals since chicken skin is high in fat.

Turkey Burgers

A low-fat alternative to regular burgers. Tasty turkey patties are irresistible when topped with grilled pineapple slices and spinach.

Lean ground turkey	1 lb.	454 g
Finely chopped red onion	1/2 cup	125 mL
Garlic cloves, minced (or 1/2 tsp., 2 mL, powder)	2	2
Fresh whole wheat bread crumbs	1/3 cup	75 mL
Chopped fresh mint leaves (or 3/4 – 2 1/4 tsp., 4 – 11 mL, dried), optional	1 – 3 tbsp.	15 – 50 mL
Low-sodium soy sauce	1 tbsp.	15 mL
Fresh (or canned, well-drained) pineapple slices	6	6
Light sour cream	3 tbsp.	50 mL
Whole cranberry sauce	3 tbsp.	50 mL
Whole wheat buns, cut in half and toasted	6	6
Fresh spinach leaves, stems removed, packed	1 1/2 cups	375 mL

Preheat barbecue to medium. Combine first 6 ingredients in large bowl until well mixed. Divide and shape into 6 patties. Place on greased grill. Close lid. Cook over medium heat for 5 to 7 minutes per side until browned and no longer pink in centre. Keep warm.

Place pineapple slices on greased grill. Close lid. Cook over medium heat for 3 to 5 minutes per side until browned.

Combine sour cream and cranberry sauce in small bowl. Spread cut sides of buns with about 1 1/2 tsp. (7 mL) sour cream mixture.

Place 1 patty on bottom half of each bun. Top with pineapple and spinach. Cover with top half of each bun. Makes 6 burgers.

1 burger: 300 Calories; 10 g Total Fat (3.7 g Mono, 2.1 g Poly, 3 g Sat); 63 mg Cholesterol; 34 g Carbohydrate; 3 g Fibre; 19 g Protein; 422 mg Sodium

1. Spinach Raspberry Salad, page 61
2. Grilled Vegetable Kabobs, page 112
3. Herb-Crusted Pork, page 118

Orange Chicken Stew

This easy all-in-one dish has a wonderful, rich and tangy sauce. Serve with steamed rice, pasta or mashed potatoes.

Bone-in, skinless chicken breast halves	3 lbs.	1.4 kg
All-purpose flour	1/4 cup	60 mL
Canola oil	1 tbsp.	15 mL
Large onion, thinly sliced	1	1
Garlic cloves, minced (or 1 tsp., 5 mL, powder)	4	4
Fresh rosemary sprigs (about 2 inch, 5 cm, lengths), or 3/4 tsp. (4 mL) dried	3	3
Prepared orange juice	1 cup	250 mL
Red (or alcohol-free) wine	1 cup	250 mL
Grainy mustard	1 tbsp.	15 mL
Pepper	1/2 tsp.	2 mL
Pitted prunes	2/3 cup	150 mL

Dredge chicken in flour to coat completely.

Sear chicken, in batches, in canola oil in large pot or Dutch oven on medium-high until browned. Return all chicken to pot.

Add next 8 ingredients. Mix well. Bring to a boil. Reduce heat to medium-low. Simmer, uncovered, for about 30 minutes, stirring occasionally, until chicken is tender and sauce is thickened. Serves 6.

1 serving: 308 Calories; 6.4 g Total Fat (2.7 g Mono, 1.6 g Poly, 1.2 g Sat); 94 mg Cholesterol; 24 g Carbohydrate; 2 g Fibre; 38 g Protein; 122 mg Sodium

1. Cognac Peach Dessert, page 136
2. Minted Peas And Beans, page 128
3. Poached Sole Rolls, page 94

Shrimp And Red Pepper Pizza

A light, California-style pizza with a whole wheat crust. For a crispier crust, use a dark pizza pan, a pan with a perforated base or a pizza stone.

WHOLE WHEAT CRUST DOUGH

Granulated sugar	1/2 tsp.	2 mL
Warm water	3/4 cup	175 mL
Active dry yeast (or 1/4 oz., 8 g, envelope)	1 tbsp.	15 mL
All-purpose flour	1 1/4 cups	300 mL
Whole wheat flour	1/2 cup	125 mL
Salt	1/2 tsp.	2 mL
Large red pepper, quartered	1	1
Roasted Tomato Sauce, page 135	1/3 cup	75 mL
Raw medium shrimp, peeled and deveined	9 oz.	255 g
Baby spinach leaves, packed	3/4 cup	175 mL
Chopped fresh sweet basil (or 3/4 – 1 1/2 tsp., 4 – 7 mL, dried)	1 – 2 tbsp.	15 – 30 mL
Finely grated fresh Parmesan cheese	1/3 cup	75 mL

Whole Wheat Crust Dough: Stir sugar into warm water in small bowl until sugar is dissolved. Sprinkle yeast over top. Let stand for 10 minutes. Stir to dissolve yeast.

Combine both flours and salt in large bowl. Stir in yeast mixture. Mix until dough just comes together. Turn out onto lightly floured surface. Knead for about 5 minutes until smooth and elastic. Place in large greased bowl, turning once to grease top. Cover with greased waxed paper and tea towel. Let stand in warm place for about 50 minutes until doubled in bulk.

Broil red pepper, skin-side up, 4 inches (10 cm) from heat for about 10 minutes until skin is blistered and blackened. Place in bowl. Cover. Let stand for 10 minutes to sweat. Peel and discard skin from pepper. Cut pepper into 1/4 inch (6 mm) thick strips.

Turn dough out onto lightly floured surface. Shape into ball. Roll out and press in lightly greased 12 inch (30 cm) pizza pan, forming rim around edge. Spread tomato sauce evenly over crust to within 1/2 inch (12 mm) of edge. Layer with shrimp, spinach, basil and red pepper. Sprinkle Parmesan cheese over top. Bake on bottom rack in 500°F (260°C) oven for about 20 minutes until crust is crispy and browned. Cuts into 8 wedges.

1 wedge: 145 Calories; 1.9 g Total Fat (0.5 g Mono, 0.3 g Poly, 0.9 g Sat); 40 mg Cholesterol; 23 g Carbohydrate; 2 g Fibre; 10 g Protein; 241 mg Sodium

Pictured on page 54.

Seafood Stew

Tender chunks of seafood in a tasty wine and tomato-based stew. Serve this with lots of crusty bread to sop up the juices.

Chopped onion	1 cup	250 mL
Garlic cloves, minced (or 1/2 tsp., 2 mL, powder)	2	2
Dried crushed chilies (optional)	1 tsp.	5 mL
Chopped red pepper	1 cup	250 mL
Pepper	1/2 tsp.	2 mL
Canola oil	2 tsp.	10 mL
Stewed Tomatoes, with juice, page 20	3 cups	750 mL
Dry white (or alcohol-free) wine	1 cup	250 mL
Chicken Stock, page 12	1 cup	250 mL
Fresh (blue) mussels, scrubbed clean	1 lb.	454 g
Halibut fillets, cut into 1 inch (2.5 cm) pieces	12 oz.	340 g
Raw medium shrimp, peeled and deveined	12 oz.	340 g
Navy Beans, page 19	1 1/2 cups	375 mL
Fresh (or frozen, thawed) scallops, halved if large	4 oz.	113 g
Chopped fresh sweet basil (or 1 1/2 – 4 tsp., 7 – 20 mL, dried)	2 – 5 tbsp.	30 – 75 mL

Sauté first 5 ingredients in canola oil in large pot or Dutch oven for about 10 minutes until onion is soft.

Add tomatoes with juice, wine and stock. Stir. Bring to a boil. Reduce heat to medium. Simmer, uncovered, for 20 to 25 minutes, stirring occasionally, until thickened.

Add next 4 ingredients. Stir. Cover. Simmer for 3 minutes.

Add scallops and basil. Stir. Cover. Simmer for about 2 minutes until scallops are opaque. Discard any unopened mussels. Makes 10 cups (2.5 L). Serves 8.

1 serving: 232 Calories; 8.4 g Total Fat (4.3 g Mono, 1.5 g Poly, 1.4 g Sat); 85 mg Cholesterol; 20 g Carbohydrate; 5 g Fibre; 20 g Protein; 250 mg Sodium

Pictured on page 53.

Poached Sole Rolls

These mild, flaky fillets of sole are wrapped around a delicious shrimp filling and then delicately poached in white wine. A wonderful dish for a special occasion.

Sole fillets (about 1 1/2 lbs., 680 g)	**8**	**8**
Light spreadable cream cheese	**1/4 cup**	**60 mL**
Chopped fresh dill (or 3/4 – 2 1/4 tsp., 4 – 11 mL, dill weed)	**1 – 3 tbsp.**	**15 – 50 mL**
Chopped green onion	**3 tbsp.**	**50 mL**
Raw medium shrimp, peeled and deveined, finely chopped	**12 oz.**	**340 g**
Dry white (or alcohol-free) wine	**3/4 cup**	**175 mL**
Water	**1/2 cup**	**125 mL**
LEMON SAUCE		
Soft tub margarine (or butter)	**1 tbsp.**	**15 mL**
All-purpose flour	**3 tbsp.**	**50 mL**
Lemon juice	**2 tbsp.**	**30 mL**

Lay fillets on work surface. Blot dry using paper towels.

Mash cream cheese, dill and green onion with fork in medium bowl until well mixed and smooth.

Add shrimp. Mix well. Spread about 2 tbsp. (30 mL) over each fillet. Roll up. Secure with wooden picks.

Combine wine and water in ungreased 2 quart (2 L) shallow casserole. Arrange rolls in single layer in wine mixture. Cover. Bake in 350°F (175°C) oven for 20 to 25 minutes until fish flakes easily when tested with fork. Gently remove fish from liquid using slotted spoon. Keep warm. Strain liquid, reserving 1 1/2 cups (375 mL).

Lemon Sauce: Melt margarine in medium saucepan on medium. Stir in flour until smooth. Heat and stir for 1 minute. Whisk in reserved liquid and lemon juice. Heat and stir for about 5 minutes until boiling and thickened. Makes about 1 cup (250 mL) sauce. Serve over fish rolls. Serves 8.

1 serving: 145 Calories; 3.2 g Total Fat (trace Mono, 0.7 g Poly, 1 g Sat); 92 mg Cholesterol; 4 g Carbohydrate; trace Fibre; 24 g Protein; 192 mg Sodium

Pictured on page 90.

Tomato Chili Mussels

Tender, steamed mussels in a tomato broth flavoured with garlic, wine, chilies and sweet basil.

Fresh (blue) mussels, scrubbed clean	**2 1/4 lbs.**	**1 kg**
Boiling water		
Finely chopped onion	**1 cup**	**250 mL**
Garlic cloves, minced (or 1 tsp., 5 mL, powder)	**4**	**4**
Dried crushed chilies	**1 tsp.**	**5 mL**
Pepper	**1/2 tsp.**	**2 mL**
Olive (or canola) oil	**1 tsp.**	**5 mL**
Roasted Tomato Sauce, page 135	**1 cup**	**250 mL**
Dry white (or alcohol-free) wine	**1/2 cup**	**125 mL**
Finely chopped fresh sweet basil (or 3/4 – 3 3/4 tsp., 4 – 19 mL, dried)	**1 – 5 tbsp.**	**15 – 75 mL**

Place mussels in large pot or Dutch oven which is 1/4 full of boiling water. Cover. Simmer, uncovered, for 3 to 5 minutes until shells are opened and mussels are tender. Drain, reserving 1/2 cup (125 mL) mussel broth. Turn mussels into medium bowl, discarding any that are unopened. Cover to keep warm.

Sauté next 4 ingredients in olive oil in same pot for about 5 minutes until onion is soft.

Add tomato sauce, wine and reserved mussel broth. Stir. Bring to a boil. Boil, uncovered, for about 10 minutes until thickened.

Add mussels and basil. Stir to coat. Serves 4.

1 serving: 132 Calories; 3.1 g Total Fat (1.2 g Mono, 0.6 g Poly, 0.5 g Sat); 19 mg Cholesterol; 12 g Carbohydrate; 2 g Fibre; 10 g Protein; 210 mg Sodium

Set reasonable goals when changing eating habits in order to improve your health. For example, add 1 fruit to your diet every other day until you are more in line with the recommendations of Canada's Food Guide.

Snapper Burgers

Fantastic fish patties with a hint of curry, garlic and onions. Top these burgers with your favourite fresh vegetables.

Chopped onion	1/2 cup	125 mL
Whole garlic cloves (or 1/4 – 1/2 tsp., 1 – 2 mL, powder)	1 – 2	1 – 2
Finely grated gingerroot (or 1/4 tsp., 1 mL, ground ginger)	1 tsp.	5 mL
Snapper fillets, coarsely chopped	1 lb.	454 g
Fresh whole wheat bread crumbs	3/4 cup	175 mL
Large egg, fork-beaten	1	1
Mild curry paste	1 1/2 tbsp.	25 mL
Low-fat plain yogurt	1/2 cup	125 mL
Finely chopped English cucumber, with peel	1/4 cup	60 mL
Whole wheat (or grain) buns, cut in half and toasted	6	6
Fresh spinach leaves, stems removed, packed	1 cup	250 mL
Medium tomatoes, sliced	2	2

Put onion, garlic and ginger into food processor. Process until finely chopped.

Add next 4 ingredients. Process until well combined and snapper is finely chopped. Do not overprocess. Shape into 6 patties. Coat large frying pan with cooking spray. Cook patties on medium for about 5 minutes per side until browned. Do not overcook.

Combine yogurt and cucumber in medium bowl.

Spread cut sides of buns with 1 tbsp. (15 mL) yogurt mixture. Place 1 patty on bottom half of each bun. Top with spinach and tomato. Cover with top half of each bun. Makes 6 burgers.

1 burger: 299 Calories; 6.1 g Total Fat (2.4 g Mono, 1.4 g Poly, 1.4 g Sat); 64 mg Cholesterol; 37 g Carbohydrate; 4 g Fibre; 25 g Protein; 399 mg Sodium

Use the barbecue or electric grill to cook meat, fish, poultry, vegetables and even fruit that is flavourful and low in fat.

Red Scallop Vermicelli

A saucy pasta dish. Tender scallops served over vermicelli noodles.

Sliced onion	**3/4 cup**	**175 mL**
Garlic cloves, minced (or 1/4 – 3/4 tsp., 1 – 4 mL, powder)	**1 – 3**	**1 – 3**
Olive (or canola) oil	**1 tsp.**	**5 mL**
Roasted Tomato Sauce, page 135	**1 cup**	**250 mL**
Water	**1/2 cup**	**125 mL**
Dry red (or alcohol-free) wine	**1/4 cup**	**60 mL**
Ripe large roma (plum) tomatoes, diced	**4**	**4**
Granulated sugar	**1/2 tsp.**	**2 mL**
Dried crushed chilies	**1/8 – 1/4 tsp.**	**0.5 – 1 mL**
Bay leaf	**1**	**1**
Fresh (or frozen, thawed) small bay scallops	**12 oz.**	**340 g**
Chopped fresh sweet basil (or 3/4 – 2 1/4 tsp., 4 – 11 mL, dried)	**1 – 4 tbsp.**	**15 – 60 mL**
Vermicelli	**8 oz.**	**225 g**
Boiling water	**10 cups**	**2.5 L**

Chopped fresh parsley, for garnish
Grated light Parmesan cheese, sprinkle

Sauté onion and garlic in olive oil in large non-stick frying pan until soft.

Add next 7 ingredients. Stir. Bring to a boil. Reduce heat to medium-low. Simmer, uncovered, for about 30 minutes until slightly thickened. Remove and discard bay leaf.

Stir in scallops and basil. Bring to a boil. Reduce heat to medium-low. Simmer, uncovered, for 2 to 3 minutes until scallops are white and slightly firm. Remove from heat. Cover to keep warm.

Cook vermicelli in boiling water in large uncovered pot or Dutch oven for 5 to 6 minutes, stirring occasionally, until tender but firm. Drain. Divide vermicelli among 4 individual bowls. Divide sauce over top.

Sprinkle with parsley and Parmesan cheese. Makes 6 1/2 cups (1.6 L). Serves 4.

1 serving: 325 Calories; 4 g Total Fat (1.4 g Mono, 1.4 g Poly, 0.5 g Sat); 14 mg Cholesterol; 56 g Carbohydrate; 5 g Fibre; 16 g Protein; 106 mg Sodium

Orange And Dill Salmon

Salmon steaks marinated in citrus juice, maple syrup, wine and dill. Barbecued to perfection.

Prepared orange juice	1/2 cup	125 mL
Maple (or maple-flavoured) syrup	1/3 cup	75 mL
Dry white (or alcohol-free) wine	1/4 cup	60 mL
Chopped fresh dill (or 1 tbsp., 15 mL, dill weed)	1/4 cup	60 mL
Low-sodium soy sauce	1 tbsp.	15 mL
Salmon steaks, 3/4 – 1 inch (2 – 2.5 cm) thick (about 4 oz., 113 g, each)	4	4

Combine first 5 ingredients in large shallow dish.

Add salmon steaks. Turn to coat. Cover. Chill for at least 4 hours or overnight, turning occasionally. Remove salmon. Discard marinade. Cook salmon on greased electric grill over medium heat for about 5 minutes per side until salmon flakes easily when tested with fork. Serves 4.

1 serving: 207 Calories; 3.7 g Total Fat (1 g Mono, 1.5 g Poly, 0.6 g Sat); 55 mg Cholesterol; 21 g Carbohydrate; trace Fibre; 22 g Protein; 210 mg Sodium

Fish Fingers

Serve these fish fingers with Red Pepper Sauce, page 134, for dipping. Also try with fat-free mayonnaise mixed with capers, finely chopped red onion and lemon juice.

All-purpose flour	1/4 cup	60 mL
Egg whites (large)	2	2
Fine dry whole wheat bread crumbs	1/2 cup	125 mL
Corn flake crumbs	1/2 cup	125 mL
Garlic powder	1/2 tsp.	2 mL
Onion powder	1/2 tsp.	2 mL
Paprika	1/2 tsp.	2 mL
Dry mustard	1/4 tsp.	1 mL
Frozen Boston bluefish fillets, thawed, cut into 1 inch (2.5 cm) strips, about 3 inches (7.5 cm) long	14 1/2 oz.	397 g

(continued on next page)

Measure flour into shallow dish.

Beat egg whites with fork in small bowl until frothy.

Combine next 6 ingredients in separate small bowl.

Dip fillets into flour to coat well. Dip into egg whites to moisten. Dip into bread crumb mixture to coat well. Arrange on greased baking sheet. Spray completely with cooking spray. Bake, uncovered, in 375°F (190°C) oven for 12 to 15 minutes, turning once, until fish flakes easily when tested with fork. Makes 10 fish fingers. Serves 4.

1 serving: 228 Calories; 5 g Total Fat (2.2 g Mono, 1.3 g Poly, 0.9 g Sat); 38 mg Cholesterol; 26 g Carbohydrate; 1 g Fibre; 18 g Protein; 316 mg Sodium

Shrimp And Rice Fritters

These simple and mildly flavoured shrimp and rice fritters are so tasty served with salsa and low-fat sour cream.

All-purpose flour	**1/2 cup**	**125 mL**
Whole wheat flour	**1/4 cup**	**60 mL**
Baking powder	**1 1/2 tsp.**	**7 mL**
Cooked brown rice (about 1/3 cup, 75 mL, uncooked)	**1 cup**	**250 mL**
Large egg, fork-beaten	**1**	**1**
Milk	**1 cup**	**250 mL**
Raw medium shrimp, peeled and deveined, chopped	**3/4 lb.**	**340 g**
Finely chopped green onion	**1/4 cup**	**60 mL**
Chopped fresh parsley (or 1 tbsp., 15 mL, flakes)	**1/4 cup**	**60 mL**
Pepper	**1/4 tsp.**	**1 mL**

Combine first 4 ingredients in large bowl.

Combine remaining 6 ingredients in medium bowl. Add to rice mixture. Stir. Heat greased non-stick frying pan on medium. Cook, using 1/4 cup (60 mL) batter for each fritter, for about 3 minutes per side until golden and shrimp is tender. Makes about 12 fritters. Serves 6.

1 serving: 162 Calories; 2.2 g Total Fat (0.7 g Mono, 0.5 g Poly, 0.8 g Sat); 104 mg Cholesterol; 22 g Carbohydrate; 2 g Fibre; 12 g Protein; 264 mg Sodium

Seafood Pasta Salad

The flavours of the shrimp and scallops in this pasta meal salad are brought out by the light gingery dressing.

Chicken Stock, page 12	1/2 cup	125 mL
Dry white (or alcohol-free) wine	1/2 cup	125 mL
Raw large shrimp, peeled and deveined	1 lb.	454 g
Raw medium scallops	7 oz.	200 g
Whole wheat penne pasta	3 cups	750 mL
Boiling water	9 cups	2.25 L
Sliced red onion	1 1/2 cups	375 mL
Can of sliced water chestnuts, drained	8 oz.	227 mL
Sliced fresh oyster mushrooms (about 7 oz., 200 g)	2 cups	500 mL
Snow peas, trimmed and sliced diagonally	2 1/3 cups	575 mL
CHILI SESAME VINAIGRETTE		
Rice wine (or white wine) vinegar	1/2 cup	125 mL
Sweet (or regular) chili sauce	3 tbsp.	50 mL
Low-sodium soy sauce	1 tbsp.	15 mL
Sesame (or canola) oil	2 tsp.	10 mL
Finely grated gingerroot (or 1/4 tsp., 1 mL, ground ginger)	1 tsp.	5 mL
Garlic clove, minced (or 1/4 tsp., 1 mL, powder)	1	1

Combine stock and wine in large pot or Dutch oven. Bring to a simmer on medium. Add shrimp and scallops. Cover. Simmer for about 3 minutes, stirring once, until scallops are just opaque and slightly firm. Drain well. Cool. Set aside.

Cook pasta in boiling water in same pot for 8 to 10 minutes, stirring occasionally, until tender but firm. Drain. Rinse under cold water. Drain well. Turn into large bowl.

Add shrimp mixture and next 4 ingredients. Stir.

Chili Sesame Vinaigrette: Combine all 6 ingredients in jar with tight-fitting lid. Shake well. Makes 2/3 cup (150 mL) vinaigrette. Pour over pasta mixture. Toss. Makes 13 cups (3.25 L). Serves 8.

1 serving: 267 Calories; 3 g Total Fat (0.8 g Mono, 1.1 g Poly, 0.5 g Sat); 71 mg Cholesterol; 44 g Carbohydrate; 7 g Fibre; 19 g Protein; 457 mg Sodium

Halibut Stir-Fry

This stir-fry is a wonderful blend of flavours and textures. Halibut works perfectly in a stir-fry as it is firm enough to hold its shape. Try this with any of your favourite vegetables.

SAUCE		
Cornstarch	1 tbsp.	15 mL
Chicken Stock, page 12	1/3 cup	75 mL
Lemon juice	1 tbsp.	15 mL
Dried whole oregano	1/2 tsp.	2 mL
Granulated sugar	1/4 tsp.	1 mL
Lemon pepper	1/4 tsp.	1 mL
Chicken Stock, page 12	2/3 cup	150 mL
Thinly sliced carrot	1 cup	250 mL
Diced butternut (or other) squash	1 cup	250 mL
Cauliflower (or broccoli) florets	1 cup	250 mL
Frozen peas	2/3 cup	150 mL
Canola oil	1 tbsp.	15 mL
Fresh (or frozen, thawed) halibut steaks	1 1/4 lbs.	560 g
(or 1 lb., 454 g, fillets), trimmed, boned and		
cut into 3/4 inch (2 cm) cubes		
Green onions, sliced	2	2

Sauce: Combine first 6 ingredients in small bowl. Set aside.

Heat second amount of stock in non-stick wok or frying pan on medium-high. Add carrot, squash and cauliflower. Cook, uncovered, for about 5 minutes, stirring once or twice, until tender-crisp.

Add peas. Heat and stir for about 2 minutes until peas are heated through. Turn into medium bowl.

Heat same wok on medium-high until hot. Add canola oil. Add halibut. Stir-fry for about 2 minutes until opaque. Stir cornstarch mixture. Add to halibut. Heat and stir for about 1 minute until boiling and thickened. Add vegetable mixture and green onion. Stir until heated through. Makes about 4 cups (1 L). Serves 4.

1 serving: 262 Calories; 7.4 g Total Fat (3.2 g Mono, 2.3 g Poly, 0.9 g Sat); 45 mg Cholesterol; 15 g Carbohydrate; 5 g Fibre; 32 g Protein; 150 mg Sodium

Honey Skewered Scallops

This sweet and spicy dish will add pizzazz and fun to your meal. The trick to keeping the scallops tender is to avoid overcooking them.

Liquid honey	1/4 cup	60 mL
Dry sherry (or Chinese cooking wine)	3 tbsp.	50 mL
Low-sodium soy sauce	2 tbsp.	30 mL
Finely grated gingerroot (or 1/4 tsp., 1 mL, ground ginger)	1 tsp.	5 mL
Chili sauce	1/2 tsp.	2 mL
Chinese five-spice powder	1/4 tsp.	1 mL
Fresh (or frozen, thawed) large scallops (about 12 oz., 340 g)	20	20
Bamboo skewers, 8 inch (20 cm) length, soaked in water for 10 minutes	4	4

Combine first 6 ingredients in large bowl.

Add scallops. Stir to coat. Cover. Marinate in refrigerator for 2 to 3 hours, stirring occasionally.

Thread 5 scallops onto each skewer. Cook on greased electric grill over medium heat for about 5 minutes, turning occasionally, until scallops are opaque. Makes 4 skewers.

1 skewer: 150 Calories; 0.7 g Total Fat (trace Mono, 0.2 g Poly, 0.1 g Sat); 29 mg Cholesterol; 21 g Carbohydrate; trace Fibre; 15 g Protein; 431 mg Sodium

Bake, broil, roast or microwave food instead of frying. Or use a non-stick frying pan with little or no oil. To further lower the fat content of food, always drain off excess fat after frying.

Spiced Lamb Stew

Tender chunks of spiced lamb in a delicious tomato-based sauce. Increase the amounts of spices for a more robust flavour.

Boneless leg of lamb, trimmed of fat, cut into cubes	**1 lb.**	**454 g**
Chopped onion	**3 cups**	**750 mL**
Garlic cloves, minced (or 1/2 – 1 tsp., 2 – 5 mL, powder)	**2 – 4**	**2 – 4**
Canola oil	**2 tsp.**	**10 mL**
Ground cumin	**2 – 3 tsp.**	**10 – 15 mL**
Ground coriander	**2 – 3 tsp.**	**10 – 15 mL**
Ground ginger	**1 – 2 tsp.**	**5 – 10 mL**
Allspice	**1/2 – 1 tsp.**	**2 – 5 mL**
Cinnamon stick (4 inch, 10 cm, length)	**1**	**1**
Whole green cardamom, bruised (see Tip, below)	**4 – 6**	**4 – 6**
Stewed Tomatoes, with juice, page 20	**2 cups**	**500 mL**
Chickpeas, page 15	**1 cup**	**250 mL**

Brown lamb, in 2 batches, in non-stick frying pan on medium-high for 5 to 10 minutes until browned. Remove from pan.

Sauté onion and garlic in canola oil in large pot or Dutch oven for about 5 minutes until onion is soft.

Add next 6 ingredients. Heat and stir for 1 to 2 minutes until fragrant.

Add lamb and tomatoes with juice. Stir. Bring to a boil. Reduce heat to low. Cover. Simmer for 1 to 1 1/2 hours, stirring occasionally, until lamb is tender. Remove and discard cinnamon and cardamom.

Add chickpeas. Heat and stir for about 5 minutes until heated through. Makes about 5 cups (1.25 L). Serves 4.

1 serving: 334 Calories; 9.7 g Total Fat (3.8 g Mono, 1.9 g Poly, 2.2 g Sat); 73 mg Cholesterol; 33 g Carbohydrate; 9 g Fibre; 30 g Protein; 196 mg Sodium

To bruise whole cardamom (also called cardamom pods) or garlic cloves, hit cardamom or garlic with a mallet or flat side of a wide knife to "bruise" or crack them open slightly.

Meatless Mushroom Ragoût

A thick, savoury mushroom and tomato ragoût flavoured with white wine and herbs. Use brown (cremini) mushrooms for a full-bodied, earthy flavour. This amount of sauce will coat nicely 16 oz. (454 g) dry pasta, cooked.

Dried shiitake mushrooms (about 1/2 cup, 125 mL)	1 oz.	28 g
Hot water	1 1/2 cups	375 mL
Garlic cloves, minced (or 1/4 – 3/4 tsp., 1 – 4 mL, powder)	1 – 3	1 – 3
Diced onion	1 cup	250 mL
Olive (or canola) oil	2 tsp.	10 mL
Sliced fresh brown (cremini), or white, mushrooms	3 cups	750 mL
Dry white (or alcohol-free) wine	1/2 cup	125 mL
Stewed Tomatoes, with juice, page 20, mashed	2 cups	500 mL
Can of tomato paste	5 1/2 oz.	156 mL
Granulated sugar	1 tbsp.	15 mL
Bay leaf	1	1
Dried sweet basil	1 – 2 tsp.	5 – 10 mL
Dried marjoram	1/2 – 1 tsp.	2 – 5 mL
Crushed dried rosemary	1/4 – 1/2 tsp.	1 – 2 mL
Pepper	1/2 tsp.	2 mL
Light sour cream	6 tbsp.	100 mL

Soak shiitake mushrooms in hot water in small bowl for 15 minutes. Strain through coffee filter or several layers of cheesecloth, reserving mushrooms and liquid. Chop mushrooms, discarding tough stems. Set aside.

Sauté garlic and onion in olive oil in large non-stick frying pan for about 2 minutes until soft. Add brown mushrooms. Cook on medium for about 8 minutes, stirring occasionally, until liquid from mushrooms has evaporated and mushrooms are beginning to brown. Add wine. Heat and stir until boiling.

Add next 8 ingredients and reserved shiitake mushrooms and liquid. Stir well. Bring to a boil. Reduce heat to medium-low. Cover. Simmer for 1 hour, stirring occasionally. Remove cover for last 15 to 20 minutes if thicker sauce is desired. Remove and discard bay leaf. Remove from heat.

Stir in sour cream just before serving. Do not boil after adding sour cream or mixture may curdle. Makes about 4 cups (1 L). Serves 4.

1 serving: 205 Calories; 4.9 g Total Fat (1.5 g Mono, 1 g Poly, 1.6 g Sat); 8 mg Cholesterol; 38 g Carbohydrate; 6 g Fibre; 8 g Protein; 176 mg Sodium

Tofu Chili Stir-Fry

Experience the wonderful, warm tastes of the Orient in this healthy and satisfying stir-fry. The tofu absorbs the flavours of the sauce so be sure to marinate for at least an hour. Add fresh chili or chili paste to spice things up a little.

Package of lower fat firm tofu, drained well	12 1/4 oz.	350 g
Sweet (or regular) chili sauce	3 tbsp.	50 mL
Dry sherry (or Chinese cooking wine)	3 tbsp.	50 mL
Low-sodium soy sauce	1 tbsp.	15 mL
Lime juice (fresh is best)	1 tbsp.	15 mL
Hoisin sauce	1 tbsp.	15 mL
Canola oil	2 tsp.	10 mL
Medium onion, cut into 12 wedges	1	1
Garlic cloves, minced (or 1/2 tsp., 2 mL, powder)	2	2
Finely grated gingerroot (or 1/4 tsp., 1 mL, ground ginger)	1 tsp.	5 mL
Medium red pepper, sliced	1	1
Chopped baby bok choy	2 cups	500 mL
Vegetable Stock, page 14	1/4 cup	60 mL
Green onions, cut into 1 inch (2.5 cm) pieces	4	4
Water	1 tbsp.	15 mL
Cornstarch	1 tbsp.	15 mL

Cut tofu into 1/2 to 3/4 inch (1.2 to 2 cm) cubes. Place on paper towel to drain.

Combine next 5 ingredients in large bowl. Add tofu. Stir to coat. Cover. Chill for 1 to 2 hours to blend flavours.

Heat canola oil in large wok or frying pan on medium-high until hot. Add next 4 ingredients. Stir-fry for about 3 minutes until red pepper is tender-crisp.

Add bok choy and stock. Stir-fry for 1 minute.

Add green onion and tofu mixture with any liquid. Stir-fry for about 2 minutes until heated through.

Stir water into cornstarch in small cup until smooth. Add to tofu mixture. Heat and stir for 1 minute until thickened. Serves 4.

1 serving: 132 Calories; 3.3 g Total Fat (1.5 g Mono, 1.2 g Poly, 0.3 g Sat); trace Cholesterol; 19 g Carbohydrate; 3 g Fibre; 7 g Protein; 715 mg Sodium

Chewy Wheat Pilaf

Enjoy the nutty, toasty flavour of cracked wheat combined with sweet squash and carrot. The green chilies add a spicy kick.

Cracked wheat	**1 cup**	**250 mL**
Chopped onion	**2/3 cup**	**150 mL**
Garlic clove, minced (or 1/4 tsp., 1 mL, powder)	**1**	**1**
Small green chili pepper, seeds removed for less heat, chopped (see Note)	**1**	**1**
Canola oil	**2 tsp.**	**10 mL**
Diced carrot	**1/2 cup**	**125 mL**
Diced butternut squash	**2 cups**	**500 mL**
Prepared orange juice	**1 cup**	**250 mL**
Chicken Stock, page 12	**1 cup**	**250 mL**
Lemon pepper	**1/2 tsp.**	**2 mL**
Chopped fresh parsley (or fresh cilantro)	**1 tbsp.**	**15 mL**

Heat and stir wheat in non-stick frying pan on medium for about 10 minutes until wheat is golden. Turn into ungreased 3 quart (3 L) casserole.

Sauté onion, garlic and chili pepper in canola oil in same frying pan for about 5 minutes until soft. Add to wheat.

Add next 5 ingredients. Stir. Cover. Bake in 375°F (190°C) oven for 45 to 60 minutes until wheat is tender and liquid is absorbed. Stir gently.

Sprinkle with parsley. Makes 4 cups (1 L).

1 cup (250 mL): 218 Calories; 3.6 g Total Fat (1.6 g Mono, 1.1 g Poly, 0.4 g Sat); 1 mg Cholesterol; 43 g Carbohydrate; 7 g Fibre; 7 g Protein; 66 mg Sodium

Note: Wear gloves when chopping chili peppers and avoid touching your eyes.

1. Crunchy Vegetable Macaroni, page 113
2. Seafood Shells Vinaigrette, page 60
3. Garlic Tomato Pasta, page 124

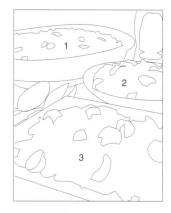

Vegetable Patties

A healthy and satisfying non-meat option for burger lovers. These patties are spiced lightly with a brown rice base. Serve with Red Pepper Sauce, page 134, or Roasted Tomato Sauce, page 135.

Finely chopped onion	1 cup	250 mL
Grated zucchini, with peel	1/2 cup	125 mL
Grated carrot	1/4 cup	60 mL
Water	1/4 cup	60 mL
Garlic clove, minced (or 1/4 tsp., 1 mL, powder)	1	1
Box of frozen chopped spinach, thawed and squeezed dry	10 oz.	300 g
Ricotta cheese	1/2 cup	125 mL
Low-sodium soy sauce	1 tbsp.	15 mL
Ground nutmeg	1/4 tsp.	1 mL
Ground ginger	1/4 tsp.	1 mL
Pepper	1/4 tsp.	1 mL
Fresh whole wheat bread crumbs	1/2 – 3/4 cup	125 – 175 mL
Cooked brown rice (about 2/3 cup, 150 mL, uncooked)	2 cups	500 mL
Egg whites (large)	2	2

Heat and stir first 5 ingredients in large frying pan on medium until simmering. Cover. Simmer for about 10 minutes, adding more water if too dry, until vegetables are tender.

Add spinach. Heat and stir for about 5 minutes until spinach is heated through. Remove from heat.

Add remaining 8 ingredients. Mix well. Shape into patties using 1/3 cup (75 mL) for each. Cook in large non-stick frying pan on medium-low for 2 to 3 minutes per side until heated through. Makes 10 patties. Serves 4.

1 serving: 277 Calories; 6.3 g Total Fat (1.9 g Mono, 0.8 g Poly, 3.2 g Sat); 16 mg Cholesterol; 43 g Carbohydrate; 6 g Fibre; 13 g Protein; 378 mg Sodium

1. Stuffed Peppers, page 123
2. Country Seed Bread, page 39
3. Grilled Asparagus, page 127
4. Steak With Spice Coating, page 77

Oriental Lentil Packets

These exotic packets are stuffed with colourful, diced vegetables and a peppery green lentil filling. Drizzle with sweet and sour sauce for a real taste adventure.

Celery rib, diced	1	1
Small carrot, cut julienne	1	1
Diced red pepper	1/2 cup	125 mL
Green onions, chopped	3	3
Garlic clove, minced (or 1/4 tsp., 1 mL, powder)	1	1
Finely grated gingerroot (or 1/4 tsp., 1 mL, ground ginger)	1 tsp.	5 mL
Canola oil	2 tsp.	10 mL
Green Lentils, page 16	1 cup	250 mL
Hoisin sauce	2 tsp.	10 mL
Low-sodium soy sauce	1 tbsp.	15 mL
Water	1/4 cup	60 mL
Sesame oil (optional)	1/2 tsp.	2 mL
Cornstarch	2 tsp.	10 mL
Dried crushed chilies	1/4 tsp.	1 mL
Rice papers	10	10
Hot water		
SWEET AND SOUR SAUCE		
Unsweetened pineapple juice	1/2 cup	125 mL
Good-For-All Ketchup, page 131	2 tbsp.	30 mL
Apple cider vinegar	1 tbsp.	15 mL
Brown sugar, packed	2 tsp.	10 mL
Cornstarch	2 tsp.	10 mL

Sauté first 6 ingredients in canola oil in large non-stick frying pan for 3 to 4 minutes until soft.

Add lentils. Stir.

Combine next 6 ingredients in small dish. Add to lentil mixture. Heat and stir on medium until boiling and slightly thickened. Cool.

Soak rice papers, 1 at a time, in hot water in shallow pie plate for 30 to 40 seconds. Place about 2 tbsp. (30 mL) filling on wrapper. Roll up, tucking in sides, to enclose filling. Repeat with remaining filling and wrappers. Line bottom of large bamboo steamer or regular steamer basket with parchment paper. Spray with cooking spray. Arrange packets in single layer, not touching. Place bamboo steamer in wok on rack, or place steamer basket in pan, over simmering water. Cover. Steam for 10 to 12 minutes until heated through.

(continued on next page)

Sweet And Sour Sauce: Combine all 5 ingredients in small saucepan. Heat and stir on medium until boiling and thickened. Makes 1/2 cup (125 mL) sauce. Spoon over packets. Serves 3 or 4.

1 serving: 323 Calories; 4 g Total Fat (2.1 g Mono, 1.3 g Poly, 0.3 g Sat); trace Cholesterol; 62 g Carbohydrate; 6 g Fibre; 9 g Protein; 258 mg Sodium

Baked Potato Dinner

A tasty variation of the baked potato. The golden, cheesy filling is flavoured with garlic, mushrooms and green onion. Add a salad or steamed vegetables to make this a complete meal.

Extra-large baking potatoes (about 3/4 lb., 340 g, each), with peel	2	2
Garlic cloves, minced (or 1/4 – 1/2 tsp., 1 – 2 mL, powder)	1 – 2	1 – 2
Sliced brown (cremini), or white, mushrooms	2 cups	500 mL
Canola oil	2 tsp.	10 mL
Green onion, sliced	1	1
Mashed soft tofu	1/2 cup	125 mL
Light Caesar salad dressing	2 tbsp.	30 mL
Chopped fresh dill (or 1/2 tsp., 2 mL, dill weed)	2 tsp.	10 mL
Coarsely ground pepper	1/16 tsp.	0.5 mL
Grated light sharp Cheddar cheese	1/2 cup	125 mL
Paprika, sprinkle		

Bake potatoes directly on centre rack in 400°F (205°C) oven for 60 to 70 minutes until tender. Cut in half lengthwise. Let stand until cool enough to handle. Spoon pulp into medium bowl, leaving shells 1/4 inch (6 mm) thick. Set shells aside. Mash potato in bowl.

Cook garlic and mushrooms in canola oil in large non-stick frying pan on medium until liquid from mushrooms has evaporated and mushrooms are golden. Add to potato.

Add next 5 ingredients. Mash.

Add cheese. Stir. Divide and spoon filling among shells. Sprinkle with paprika. Place in ungreased shallow 2 quart (2 L) casserole. Bake, uncovered, in 400°F (205°C) oven for about 30 minutes until heated through. Makes 4 stuffed potatoes.

1 stuffed potato: 301 Calories; 4.8 g Total Fat (1.9 g Mono, 1.5 g Poly, 1 g Sat); 3 mg Cholesterol; 55 g Carbohydrate; 5 g Fibre; 11 g Protein; 195 mg Sodium

Grilled Vegetable Kabobs

These kabobs are an easy, versatile summer treat. Serve on their own or with couscous or rice.
Substitute the eggplant with small white mushrooms if desired.

Finely grated lemon zest	1 tsp.	5 mL
Roasted Tomato Sauce, page 135	1 cup	250 mL
Freshly squeezed lemon juice (about 1 small lemon)	1/4 cup	60 mL
Liquid honey	3 tbsp.	50 mL
Low-sodium soy sauce	1 tbsp.	15 mL
Small green chili pepper, seeds removed for less heat, finely chopped (see Note)	1	1
Ground allspice	1/2 tsp.	2 mL
Medium onions, cut into 6 wedges each	2	2
Medium zucchini (about 1 1/2 lbs., 680 g), with peel, cut into 1 inch (2.5 cm) slices	4	4
Cherry tomatoes	24	24
Medium eggplant (about 1 lb., 454 g), cut into 1 inch (2.5 cm) cubes	1	1
Medium red peppers, cut into 1 inch (2.5 cm) pieces	2	2
Bamboo skewers, 8 inch (20 cm) length, soaked in water for 10 minutes	12	12

Combine first 7 ingredients in large bowl.

Add next 5 ingredients. Toss to coat. Cover. Chill for 1 to 2 hours.

Thread vegetables, in order listed above, onto skewers, reserving marinade. Cook on greased electric grill over medium-low heat for 10 to 15 minutes, turning and brushing with reserved marinade, until vegetables are tender and browned. Makes 12 kabobs. Serves 6.

1 serving: 136 Calories; 0.7 g Total Fat (0 g Mono, 0.3 g Poly, 0.1 g Sat); 0 mg Cholesterol; 33 g Carbohydrate; 6 g Fibre; 4 g Protein; 117 mg Sodium

Pictured on front cover and on page 89.

Note: Wear gloves when chopping chili peppers and avoid touching your eyes.

Crunchy Vegetable Macaroni

A simple and colourful macaroni dish with lightly steamed vegetables and a zesty cheese flavour. Serve with a tossed salad or Bruschetta, page 29.

Water	2 1/2 cups	625 mL
Thinly sliced carrot	1/3 cup	75 mL
Fresh asparagus, cut into 1 inch (2.5 cm) pieces	1 1/2 cups	375 mL
Sugar snap peas	1 cup	250 mL
Diced red pepper	1/4 cup	60 mL
Ice water		
Can of skim evaporated milk	13 1/2 oz.	385 mL
Garlic and herb no-salt seasoning (such as Mrs. Dash)	1 tsp.	5 mL
Lemon pepper	1/2 tsp.	2 mL
Whole wheat elbow macaroni, uncooked	2 cups	500 mL
Green onions, finely sliced	2	2
Grated light sharp Cheddar cheese (about 4 oz., 113 g)	1 cup	250 mL
Chopped fresh parsley, for garnish	2 tbsp.	30 mL

Bring water to a boil in medium saucepan. Add carrot. Cover. Cook on medium for 4 minutes. Add asparagus, peas and red pepper. Cover. Cook for 3 minutes. Remove vegetables with slotted spoon to ice water to cool quickly, reserving 2 cups (500 mL) cooking water. Drain vegetables once cooled. Set aside.

Add evaporated milk, seasoning and lemon pepper to reserved cooking water in same saucepan. Bring to a boil. Add macaroni. Cook, uncovered, on medium for about 15 minutes, stirring frequently, until macaroni is tender and most liquid is absorbed. Do not drain. Pour into large bowl.

Add asparagus mixture, green onion and cheese. Stir. Turn into greased 3 quart (3 L) casserole. Cover. Bake in 350°F (175°C) oven for about 30 minutes until heated through.

Garnish with parsley. Makes 8 cups (2 L). Serves 4.

1 serving: 284 Calories; 3 g Total Fat (0.8 g Mono, 0.3 g Poly, 1.4 g Sat); 10 mg Cholesterol; 44 g Carbohydrate; 6 g Fibre; 22 g Protein; 366 mg Sodium

Pictured on page 107.

Pesto And Tomato Pizza

Serve this thin, crispy-crust pizza with a green salad for a delicious, healthy meal.

CRUST

Warm water	1/3 cup	75 mL
Granulated sugar	1/2 tsp.	2 mL
Active dry yeast	2 tsp.	10 mL
All-purpose flour	1/2 cup	125 mL
Whole wheat flour	1/4 cup	60 mL
Salt	1/2 tsp.	2 mL

TOPPING

Pesto, page 132	1/4 cup	60 mL
Large ripe tomato, sliced	1	1
Sliced brown (cremini), or white, mushrooms	1 cup	250 mL
Red Pepper Sauce, page 134	1/4 cup	60 mL
Finely grated fresh Parmesan cheese	3 tbsp.	50 mL

Crust: Stir water and sugar in small bowl until sugar is dissolved. Sprinkle yeast over top. Let stand for 10 minutes. Stir to dissolve yeast.

Combine both flours and salt in large bowl. Stir in yeast mixture. Mix until dough just comes together. Turn out onto lightly floured surface. Knead for about 5 minutes until smooth and elastic. Place dough in large greased bowl, turning once to grease top. Cover with greased waxed paper and tea towel. Let stand in oven with light on and door closed for about 1 1/4 hours until doubled in bulk. Punch dough down. Turn out onto lightly floured surface. Shape into ball. Roll out and press in lightly greased 12 inch (30 cm) pizza pan, forming rim around edge.

Topping: Spread pesto evenly over crust to within 1/2 inch (12 mm) of edge. Layer with tomato and mushrooms. Spoon dollops of sauce over top. Sprinkle with Parmesan cheese. Bake on bottom rack in 500°F (260°C) oven for about 15 minutes until crust is browned and crispy. Cuts into 8 wedges.

1 wedge: 76 Calories; 1.5 g Total Fat (0.4 g Mono, 0.2 g Poly, 0.8 g Sat); 3 mg Cholesterol; 12 g Carbohydrate; 2 g Fibre; 4 g Protein; 189 mg Sodium

Mushroom Pies

Golden brown mashed potatoes with a luscious layer of rich gravy, flavoured with white wine and sweet basil. Perfect on a cold winter night!

Sliced brown (or white) mushrooms (about 1 1/2 lbs., 680 g)	**10 cups**	**2.5 L**
Medium leek (white and tender parts only), thinly sliced	**1**	**1**
Finely chopped carrot	**1 1/2 cups**	**375 mL**
Chopped celery	**1/4 cup**	**60 mL**
Canola oil	**2 tsp.**	**10 mL**
All-purpose flour	**2 tbsp.**	**30 mL**
Dry white (or alcohol-free) wine	**1/2 cup**	**125 mL**
Milk	**1 1/2 cups**	**375 mL**
Chopped fresh sweet basil (or 3/4 – 3 tsp., 4 – 15 mL, dried)	**1 – 4 tbsp.**	**15 – 60 mL**
Mashed potato (about 3 large cooked potatoes)	**4 cups**	**1 L**
Grated part-skim mozzarella cheese	**1/4 cup**	**60 mL**

Cook mushrooms, in 2 batches, in large non-stick frying pan on medium-high for 8 to 10 minutes, stirring occasionally, until lightly browned. Remove from pan to medium bowl. Set aside.

Sauté leek, carrot and celery in canola oil in same frying pan for about 10 minutes until vegetables are tender.

Sprinkle flour over leek mixture. Heat and stir for 1 to 2 minutes until vegetables are coated. Add wine. Heat and stir for about 1 minute until thickened.

Gradually stir in milk. Heat and stir for about 10 minutes until boiling and thickened. Remove from heat.

Add mushrooms and basil. Stir. Fill four 2 cup (500 mL) ramekins about 1/2 full.

Divide and spread potato over mushroom mixture. Sprinkle each with 1 tbsp. (15 mL) cheese. Bake in 425°F (220°C) oven for 10 to 15 minutes until heated through. Makes 4 pies.

1 pie: 283 Calories; 5 g Total Fat (1.9 g Mono, 0.9 g Poly, 1.6 g Sat); 10 mg Cholesterol; 45 g Carbohydrate; 5 g Fibre; 13 g Protein; 132 mg Sodium

Vegetable Chickpea Curry

A mild chickpea curry with a colourful mix of vegetables and a hint of lemon. Delicious served over couscous or brown rice.

Medium onion, quartered	1	1
Garlic cloves, peeled	2	2
Finely chopped gingerroot (or 1/2 tsp., 2 mL, ground ginger)	2 tsp.	10 mL
Curry paste	2 tsp.	10 mL
Chicken Stock, page 12	1/4 cup	60 mL
Canola oil	2 tsp.	10 mL
Chicken Stock, page 12	3/4 cup	175 mL
Diced red baby potato, with peel	1 cup	250 mL
Chickpeas, page 15	1 cup	250 mL
California vegetable mix	1 1/2 cups	375 mL
Frozen peas	1/2 cup	125 mL
Low-fat lemon yogurt	3/4 cup	175 mL
Medium tomato, seeded and diced	1	1

Process first 5 ingredients in food processor until puréed.

Heat canola oil in large non-stick frying pan on medium-high. Add onion mixture. Cook for about 5 minutes, stirring frequently, until mixture is very soft and liquid has evaporated.

Add second amount of stock and potato. Bring to a boil. Reduce heat to medium-low. Cover. Simmer for about 10 minutes until potato is tender but firm. Remove cover. Increase heat to medium-high. Boil, uncovered, for 5 to 6 minutes, stirring several times, until liquid is reduced and potato is soft.

Add chickpeas, mixed vegetables and peas. Stir. Cover. Cook on medium for 5 to 6 minutes, stirring occasionally, until vegetables are soft.

Add yogurt and tomato. Heat and stir until heated through. Makes 3 1/2 cups (875 mL). Serves 2 or 3.

1 serving: 431 Calories; 9.3 g Total Fat (3.9 g Mono, 2.7 g Poly, 1.7 g Sat); 6 mg Cholesterol; 70 g Carbohydrate; 17 g Fibre; 21 g Protein; 162 mg Sodium

Ginger Pork Stir-Fry

Strips of tender pork and fresh vegetables are coated with a wonderful ginger flavour in this fantastic stir-fry.

TANGY SAUCE

Granulated sugar	**1/4 cup**	**60 mL**
Cornstarch	**1 tbsp.**	**15 mL**
Water	**1/4 cup**	**60 mL**
Red wine vinegar	**2 tbsp.**	**30 mL**
Lemon juice	**2 tbsp.**	**30 mL**
Low-sodium soy sauce	**1 tbsp.**	**15 mL**
Sesame oil (optional)	**1 tsp.**	**5 mL**
Pork tenderloin, partially frozen, cut julienne	**3/4 – 1 lb.**	**340 – 454 g**
Finely grated gingerroot (or 1/4 – 3/4 tsp., 1 – 4 mL, ground ginger)	**1 – 3 tsp.**	**5 – 15 mL**
Garlic clove, minced (or 1/4 tsp., 1 mL, powder)	**1**	**1**
Dried crushed chilies	**1/4 tsp.**	**1 mL**
Medium carrots, thinly sliced diagonally	**2**	**2**
Small onion, cut lengthwise into 8 wedges	**1**	**1**
Bok choy, cut into 1/2 inch (12 mm) slices, packed	**4 cups**	**1 L**
Sesame seeds (optional), toasted (see Tip, page 29)	**1 tsp.**	**5 mL**

Tangy Sauce: Combine first 6 ingredients in small dish. Set aside.

Spray non-stick wok or frying pan with cooking spray. Heat on medium-high until very hot. Add sesame oil, pork, ginger, garlic and chilies. Stir-fry for about 5 minutes until beginning to brown.

Add carrot, onion and bok choy. Stir-fry for about 8 minutes until carrot is tender-crisp. Push pork mixture up side of wok, making small well in centre. Stir sauce. Pour into well. Cook for about 2 minutes, stirring in centre first and then with pork mixture, until boiling and thickened.

Sprinkle with sesame seeds. Serves 4.

1 serving: 209 Calories; 3.6 g Total Fat (1.4 g Mono, 0.5 g Poly, 1.1 g Sat); 50 mg Cholesterol; 23 g Carbohydrate; 2 g Fibre; 20 g Protein; 241 mg Sodium

Herb-Crusted Pork

Sweet, citrus-flavoured sauce complements the flavours of the sage and parsley in the herb crust.
Serve with Yam And Parsnip Mash, page 121.

Prepared orange juice	**1/2 cup**	**125 mL**
Dry white (or alcohol-free) wine	**1/2 cup**	**125 mL**
Liquid honey	**2 tbsp.**	**30 mL**
Garlic cloves, minced (or 1/2 tsp., 2 mL, powder)	**2**	**2**
Pork tenderloin, visible fat removed	**1 lb.**	**454 g**
Grainy mustard	**1 1/2 tbsp.**	**25 mL**
Chopped fresh parsley (or 3 – 3 1/2 tsp., 15 – 17 mL, flakes)	**1/4 – 1/3 cup**	**60 – 75 mL**
Chopped fresh sage (or 1 1/2 tsp., 7 mL, dried)	**2 tbsp.**	**30 mL**
Coarsely ground pepper	**1 tbsp.**	**15 mL**

Combine first 4 ingredients in medium bowl. Add pork. Turn to coat. Cover. Marinate in refrigerator for at least 4 hours or overnight, turning several times. Remove pork, reserving marinade.

Spread mustard over pork.

Combine parsley, sage and pepper in shallow dish. Roll pork in herb mixture to coat completely. Spray with cooking spray. Place pork on greased wire rack on baking sheet. Bake in 375°F (190°C) oven for 45 to 50 minutes until tender. Let stand for 10 minutes. Cut into 1 inch (2.5 cm) slices. Put reserved marinade into medium frying pan. Bring to a boil on medium-high. Boil for 5 to 7 minutes until slightly reduced and thickened. Serve with pork. Serves 4.

1 serving: 210 Calories; 4.7 g Total Fat (1.9 g Mono, 0.5 g Poly, 1.5 g Sat); 67 mg Cholesterol; 16 g Carbohydrate; 1 g Fibre; 25 g Protein; 154 mg Sodium

Pictured on page 89.

To add flavour to meats without adding fat, use spice rubs and vinegar or citrus-based marinades instead of heavier oil-based marinades.

Barley Risotto

A rich and versatile risotto that will accompany steak or lamb perfectly.

Brown (cremini), or white, mushrooms, sliced	3 cups	750 mL
Vegetable Stock, page 14	6 cups	1.5 L
Finely chopped onion	1 cup	250 mL
Garlic cloves, minced (or 1/4 – 1 tsp., 1 – 5 mL, powder)	1 – 4	1 – 4
Olive (or canola) oil	2 tsp.	10 mL
Red (or alcohol-free) wine	1/2 cup	125 mL
Pearl barley	1 cup	250 mL
Raisins, chopped	2/3 cup	150 mL
Chopped fresh parsley (or 1 tbsp., 15 mL, flakes)	1/4 cup	60 mL
Coarsely ground pepper	1/4 tsp.	1 mL
Finely grated fresh Parmesan cheese	1/4 cup	60 mL

Cook mushrooms in large non-stick frying pan on medium-high for 8 to 10 minutes until mushrooms are browned. Set aside.

Bring stock to a boil in medium saucepan. Reduce heat to very low. Cover.

Sauté onion and garlic in olive oil in large saucepan for about 5 minutes until onion is soft.

Add wine. Bring to a boil on medium-high. Add barley. Reduce heat to medium. Heat and stir until wine is absorbed. Gradually stir in hot stock, 1 cup (250 mL) at a time, until stock is absorbed after each addition. Add raisins during second last addition of stock. This should take about 45 minutes until stock is completely absorbed and barley is tender. Remove from heat.

Add parsley, pepper, Parmesan cheese and mushrooms. Stir. Serve immediately. Makes 4 cups (1 L).

1 cup (250 mL): 370 Calories; 5.9 g Total Fat (2.4 g Mono, 0.8 g Poly, 1.8 g Sat); 5 mg Cholesterol; 72 g Carbohydrate; 11 g Fibre; 13 g Protein; 160 mg Sodium

Glazed Winter Vegetables

Colourful vegetables tossed and baked in a sweet maple sauce. Serve with roasted chicken, beef or lamb for a delectable dinner.

Medium yam (or sweet potato), about 1 1/2 lbs. (680 g), cut into 1 inch (2.5 cm) pieces	1	1
Medium parsnips (about 1 lb., 454 g), halved lengthwise and cut into 2 inch (5 cm) pieces	4	4
Medium carrots, halved lengthwise and cut into 2 inch (5 cm) pieces	3	3
Unpeeled garlic cloves, bruised (see Tip, page 103)	4	4
Sprigs of fresh rosemary (about 2 inch, 5 cm, lengths), or 1 tsp. (5 mL) dried	4	4
Coarsely ground pepper	1/2 tsp.	2 mL
Ground cumin (optional)	1/4 – 1/2 tsp.	1 – 2 mL
Maple (or maple-flavoured) syrup	1/4 cup	60 mL

Combine all 8 ingredients in large bowl. Spray with cooking spray. Toss to coat. Arrange in single layer on greased baking sheet. Bake in 375°F (190°C) oven for about 50 minutes, stirring occasionally, until vegetables are browned and tender. Remove and discard garlic and rosemary sprigs. Serves 8.

1 serving: 148 Calories; 0.6 g Total Fat (0.2 g Mono, 0.2 g Poly, 0.1 g Sat); 0 mg Cholesterol; 35 g Carbohydrate; 6 g Fibre; 2 g Protein; 175 mg Sodium

Curry Tomato Lentils

A warm side dish to serve with curry, grilled meat or poultry. The more ripe the tomatoes, the better the flavour and texture of the dish. Try with a drizzle of low-fat yogurt.

Chopped red onion	3/4 cup	175 mL
Garlic cloves, minced (or 1/2 tsp., 2 mL, powder)	2	2
Olive (or canola) oil	2 tsp.	10 mL
Curry powder	1 tbsp.	15 mL
Ripe medium tomatoes, chopped	4	4
Green Lentils, page 16	2 cups	500 mL
Granulated sugar	1 tsp.	5 mL

(continued on next page)

Chopped fresh parsley (or 1 tbsp., 15 mL, flakes)	1/4 cup	60 mL
Lemon juice	2 tbsp.	30 mL
Pepper	1/2 tsp.	2 mL

Sauté onion and garlic in olive oil in large non-stick frying pan for about 5 minutes until onion is soft.

Add curry powder. Heat and stir for about 1 minute until fragrant.

Add tomato, lentils and sugar. Cook for 5 to 10 minutes, stirring occasionally, until tomato is soft and mixture is heated through.

Add parsley, lemon juice and pepper. Stir. Makes about 4 cups (1 L).

1/2 cup (125 mL): 98 Calories; 1.6 g Total Fat (0.9 g Mono, 0.1 g Poly, 0.2 g Sat); 0 mg Cholesterol; 17 g Carbohydrate; 4 g Fibre; 5 g Protein; 10 mg Sodium

Yam And Parsnip Mash

A warm, hearty side dish with a pleasing parsnip flavour. Complements roast beef, pork or turkey. Serve with Herb-Crusted Pork, page 118.

Large yam (or sweet potato), about 1 1/2 lbs. (680 g), peeled and chopped	1	1
Medium parsnips (about 1 lb., 454 g), chopped	4	4
Water		
Light sour cream	3 tbsp.	50 mL
Chopped fresh parsley (or 1 tbsp., 15 mL, flakes)	1/4 cup	60 mL
Finely chopped green onion	1/4 cup	60 mL
Pepper	1/2 tsp.	2 mL

Cook yam and parsnip in water in large saucepan on medium-high for about 20 minutes until tender. Drain well. Mash until smooth.

Add remaining 4 ingredients. Stir until well combined. Makes about 4 cups (1 L).

1/2 cup (125 mL): 100 Calories; 0.8 g Total Fat (0.1 g Mono, 0.1 g Poly, 0.5 g Sat); 2 mg Cholesterol; 23 g Carbohydrate; 5 g Fibre; 2 g Protein; 21 mg Sodium

Beans With Roasted Squash

Cubes of mildly spiced and sweetened squash are mixed with beans and spinach. Wonderful served with grilled chicken or pork.

Cubed butternut squash, 1/2 inch (12 mm) pieces	3 cups	750 mL
Olive (or canola) oil	2 tsp.	10 mL
Chopped onion	1 1/2 cups	375 mL
Garlic cloves, minced (or 1/2 tsp., 2 mL, powder)	2	2
Olive (or canola) oil	1 tsp.	5 mL
Ground cumin	1/4 – 1 tsp.	1 – 5 mL
Pepper	1/2 tsp.	2 mL
Liquid honey	2 tbsp.	30 mL
Freshly squeezed (or prepared) orange juice (about 2 large oranges)	3/4 cup	175 mL
Navy Beans, page 19	2 cups	500 mL
Baby spinach leaves	2 1/2 cups	625 mL

Combine squash and first amount of olive oil in large bowl. Toss to coat well. Spread on ungreased baking sheet. Roast in 375°F (190°C) oven for about 20 minutes until just soft.

Cook onion and garlic in second amount of olive oil in large non-stick frying pan or wok on medium-low for about 15 minutes until onion is soft and golden brown.

Add cumin. Heat and stir for about 1 minute until fragrant. Add squash and pepper. Mix gently until well combined.

Add honey and orange juice. Increase heat to medium-high. When beginning to boil, add beans and spinach. Heat and stir for about 3 minutes until beans are hot, spinach is wilted and liquid is mostly absorbed. Makes about 5 1/2 cups (1.4 L).

1/2 cup (125 mL): 104 Calories; 1.6 g Total Fat (1 g Mono, 0.2 g Poly, 0.2 g Sat); 0 mg Cholesterol; 20 g Carbohydrate; 4 g Fibre; 4 g Protein; 10 mg Sodium

To reduce sodium in your diet, avoid processed or packaged foods, especially soups and soup mixes. Some other foods to avoid are potato chips, salted nuts and processed deli meats.

Stuffed Peppers

These stuffed peppers are truly beautiful and make a great side dish to barbecued steak or poultry.

RICE FILLING		
Finely chopped onion	3/4 cup	175 mL
Garlic cloves, minced (or 1/2 tsp., 2 mL, powder)	2	2
Olive (or canola) oil	1 tsp.	5 mL
Ground paprika	1 tsp.	5 mL
Ground cumin (optional)	1/4 – 1 tsp.	1 – 5 mL
Ground allspice	1/4 – 1/2 tsp.	1 – 2 mL
Brown converted rice, uncooked	3/4 cup	175 mL
Vegetable Stock, page 14	1 3/4 cups	425 mL
Ripe medium roma (plum) tomatoes, chopped	3	3
Chopped raisins	1/3 cup	75 mL
Chopped dried apricots	1/3 cup	75 mL
Sliced almonds, toasted (see Tip, page 29)	1/3 cup	75 mL
Chopped fresh parsley (or 3/4 – 3 tsp., 4 – 15 mL, flakes)	1 – 4 tbsp.	15 – 60 mL
Chopped fresh sweet basil (or 3/4 – 3 tsp., 4 – 15 mL, dried)	1 – 4 tbsp.	15 – 60 mL
Medium red peppers	6	6

Rice Filling: Sauté onion and garlic in olive oil in large non-stick saucepan for about 5 minutes until soft.

Add paprika, cumin and allspice. Heat and stir for about 1 minute until fragrant.

Add rice and stock. Stir. Bring to a boil. Reduce heat to medium-low. Cover. Simmer for about 25 minutes until rice is tender. Remove from heat.

Add next 6 ingredients. Mix well. Let stand for about 5 minutes until any remaining liquid is absorbed and tomato is hot. Makes 5 cups (1.25 L) filling.

Slice tops off red peppers and reserve. Discard cores, seeds and ribs. Arrange peppers, cut side up, in lightly greased 2 quart (2 L) casserole. Spoon about 3/4 cup (175 mL) filling into each pepper. Replace tops. Bake, uncovered, in 350°F (175°C) oven for about 40 minutes until peppers are tender. Makes 6 stuffed peppers.

1 stuffed pepper: 231 Calories; 4.9 g Total Fat (2.5 g Mono, 1.2 g Poly, 0.5 g Sat); 0 mg Cholesterol; 44 g Carbohydrate; 6 g Fibre; 6 g Protein; 21 mg Sodium

Pictured on front cover and on back cover and on page 108.

Garlic Tomato Pasta

A light-tasting pasta with lots of fresh tomato and parsley. Goes well with a salad and barbecued steak or chicken.

Whole wheat penne pasta	**2 cups**	**500 mL**
Boiling water	**8 cups**	**2 L**
Sliced red onion	**1 cup**	**250 mL**
Garlic cloves, minced (or 3/4 tsp., 4 mL, powder)	**3**	**3**
Olive (or canola) oil	**2 tsp.**	**10 mL**
Chili paste (sambal oelek)	**1 tsp.**	**5 mL**
Balsamic vinegar	**1 tbsp.**	**15 mL**
Cherry (or grape) tomatoes (about 24), halved	**12 oz.**	**340 g**
Chopped fresh parsley (or 2 tbsp., 30 mL, flakes)	**1/2 cup**	**125 mL**
Finely grated fresh Parmesan cheese	**1/4 cup**	**60 mL**

Cook pasta in boiling water in large uncovered pot or Dutch oven for about 15 minutes, stirring occasionally, until tender but firm. Drain. Return to pot.

Sauté onion and garlic in olive oil in large frying pan for about 5 minutes until onion is soft.

Add next 4 ingredients. Heat and stir for about 5 minutes until tomato is just wilted. Add to pasta. Stir.

Add Parmesan cheese. Mix well. Makes 4 cups (1 L).

1 cup (250 mL): 259 Calories; 5.3 g Total Fat (2.4 g Mono, 0.7 g Poly, 1.7 g Sat); 5 mg Cholesterol; 45 g Carbohydrate; 6 g Fibre; 12 g Protein; 170 mg Sodium

Pictured on page 107.

1. Calabacitas, page 130
2. Chicken Meatballs, page 83
3. Rhubarb Crumble, page 141

Grilled Asparagus

Fresh asparagus spears are tossed with orange, honey and dill and grilled lightly. Adjust amount of chili to suit your taste. A colourful, summer side dish that will accompany any meal.

Ingredient	Imperial	Metric
Fresh asparagus spears, trimmed of tough ends	**1 lb.**	**454 g**
Finely grated orange zest	**1/2 tsp.**	**2 mL**
Freshly squeezed (or prepared) orange juice (about 2 small oranges)	**1/2 cup**	**125 mL**
Liquid honey	**2 tbsp.**	**30 mL**
Chopped fresh dill (or 3/4 – 1 1/2 tsp., 4 – 7 mL, dill weed)	**1 – 2 tbsp.**	**15 – 30 mL**
Chili paste (sambal oelek)	**1 tsp.**	**5 mL**
Ground ginger	**1 tsp.**	**5 mL**
Pepper	**1/2 tsp.**	**2 mL**
Garlic clove, minced (or 1/4 tsp., 1 mL, powder)	**1**	**1**

Spray asparagus with cooking spray. Cook on greased electric grill over medium-high heat for about 10 minutes, turning occasionally, until tender-crisp. Cooking time will vary according to thickness of asparagus spears.

Combine remaining 8 ingredients in large shallow dish. Add asparagus. Toss to coat. Cover. Chill for at least 2 hours or overnight. Remove asparagus. Discard marinade. Serve cold or at room temperature. Serves 4.

1 serving: 78 Calories; 0.8 g Total Fat (0.4 g Mono, 0.2 g Poly, 0.1 g Sat); 0 mg Cholesterol; 16 g Carbohydrate; 2 g Fibre; 2 g Protein; 34 mg Sodium

Pictured on page 108.

1. Kiwifruit Sorbet, page 139
2. Crisp Meringue Cream Pies, page 149
3. Angelic Berry Dessert, page 146

Orange Roasted Beets

These tender beets are baked and tossed in a sweet orange and maple sauce. A great side dish to serve with poultry.

Medium beets, with peel, scrubbed clean and trimmed (see Note)	**8**	**8**
Orange marmalade	**3 tbsp.**	**50 mL**
Maple (or maple-flavoured) syrup	**3 tbsp.**	**50 mL**
Prepared orange juice	**2 tbsp.**	**30 mL**
Sesame seeds, toasted (see Tip, page 29)	**2 tsp.**	**10 mL**

Wrap beets individually in foil. Place on baking sheet or directly on oven rack. Bake in 350°F (175°C) oven for about 1 hour until tender. Remove foil. Let stand for 5 minutes to cool slightly. Peel beets. Cut into quarters.

Combine marmalade, maple syrup and orange juice in medium non-stick frying pan. Heat and stir on medium-high for 3 to 5 minutes until mixture is thickened. Add beets. Toss to coat.

Sprinkle with sesame seeds. Serves 4 to 6.

1 serving: 167 Calories; 1.1 g Total Fat (0.4 g Mono, 0.4 g Poly, 0.2 g Sat); 0 mg Cholesterol; 39 g Carbohydrate; 3 g Fibre; 3 g Protein; 132 mg Sodium

Note: To prevent hands from staining, wear rubber gloves while handling beets.

Minted Peas And Beans

Crisp sugar snap peas are tossed with beans and fresh garden mint. A high-protein side dish that is succulent when served with roast lamb or pork.

Chicken Stock, page 12	**1/2 cup**	**125 mL**
Finely chopped red onion	**1/2 cup**	**125 mL**
Sugar snap peas (about 4 cups, 1 L)	**14 oz.**	**395 g**
Navy Beans, page 19	**2/3 cup**	**150 mL**
Finely chopped fresh mint leaves (or 3/4 – 2 1/4 tsp., 4 – 11 mL, dried)	**1 – 3 tbsp.**	**15 – 50 mL**
Pepper	**1/4 tsp.**	**1 mL**
Soft tub margarine	**1 tsp.**	**5 mL**

(continued on next page)

Heat stock in large frying pan on medium-high. Add red onion. Cook for about 5 minutes until onion is soft.

Add next 4 ingredients. Heat and stir for about 3 minutes until peas are tender-crisp and beans are heated through.

Add margarine. Toss until melted. Makes about 3 1/2 cups (875 mL).

1/2 cup (125 mL): 74 Calories; 0.4 g Total Fat (0.1 g Mono, 0.2 g Poly, 0.1 g Sat); trace Cholesterol; 14 g Carbohydrate; 4 g Fibre; 4 g Protein; 85 mg Sodium

Pictured on page 90.

Creamy Polenta

Serve with grilled or roast beef, pork or poultry. This polenta makes a nice change from mashed potatoes or rice.

Finely chopped onion	**3/4 cup**	**175 mL**
Olive (or canola) oil	**1 tsp.**	**5 mL**
Chicken Stock, page 12 (or Vegetable Stock, page 14)	**4 cups**	**1 L**
Yellow cornmeal	**1 1/2 cups**	**375 mL**
Light sour cream	**1/4 cup**	**60 mL**
Finely grated fresh Parmesan cheese	**1/4 cup**	**60 mL**
Pepper	**1/2 tsp.**	**2 mL**

Sauté onion in olive oil in large saucepan for about 5 minutes until soft.

Add stock. Reduce heat to medium-low. Slowly pour in cornmeal, stirring constantly. Reduce heat to low. Stir for about 25 minutes until mixture is thickened. Remove from heat.

Add sour cream, Parmesan cheese and pepper. Mix well. Makes 4 1/2 cups (1.1 L).

1/2 cup (125 mL): 132 Calories; 3.5 g Total Fat (0.8 g Mono, 0.3 g Poly, 1.3 g Sat); 6 mg Cholesterol; 21 g Carbohydrate; 2 g Fibre; 6 g Protein; 70 mg Sodium

Calabacitas

This crunchy, salsa-like side dish (pronounced cah-lah-bah-SEE-tahs) is Mexican in origin and means "little squash". It's delicious either with or without cheese and is a wonderful complement to barbecued entrees and grilled or poached fish.

Chopped onion	**3/4 cup**	**175 mL**
Jalapeño pepper, seeded and finely diced (about 2 tbsp., 30 mL), see Note	**1**	**1**
Garlic cloves, minced (or 1/2 tsp., 2 mL, powder)	**2**	**2**
Canola oil	**2 tsp.**	**10 mL**
Stewed Tomatoes, with juice, page 20 (or Roasted Tomato Sauce, page 135)	**1 cup**	**250 mL**
Granulated sugar	**1/2 tsp.**	**2 mL**
Pepper	**1/8 tsp.**	**0.5 mL**
Small zucchini (about 6 inches, 15 cm, long), with peel, sliced 1/8 inch (3 mm) thick (about 4 cups, 1 L)	**4**	**4**
Fresh (or frozen) kernel corn	**1 cup**	**250 mL**
Grated light sharp Cheddar cheese (optional)	**1/2 cup**	**125 mL**
Chopped fresh cilantro (or fresh parsley), optional		

Cook onion, jalapeño pepper and garlic in canola oil in large non-stick frying pan on medium for 3 to 4 minutes, stirring frequently to prevent browning, until soft.

Add tomatoes with juice, sugar and pepper. Mash tomatoes slightly with fork. Bring to a boil. Reduce heat. Simmer, uncovered, for about 8 minutes, stirring frequently, until mixture is thickened.

Add zucchini and corn. Stir. Cover. Cook on medium for 6 to 8 minutes until zucchini is tender. Turn into serving bowl.

Sprinkle with cheese and cilantro. Makes 4 cups (1 L). Serves 8.

1 serving: 55 Calories; 1.5 g Total Fat (0.7 g Mono, 0.5 g Poly, 0.1 g Sat); 0 mg Cholesterol; 10 g Carbohydrate; 2 g Fibre; 2 g Protein; 33 mg Sodium

Pictured on page 125.

Note: Wear gloves when chopping jalapeño peppers and avoid touching your eyes.

Good-For-All Ketchup

You won't go back to store-bought ketchup after trying this one. Try as an ingredient in marinades for grilled chicken or beef.

Tomato juice	2 cups	500 mL
Can of tomato sauce	7 1/2 oz.	213 mL
Can of tomato paste	5 1/2 oz.	156 mL
White vinegar	1/4 cup	60 mL
Granulated sugar	2 tbsp.	30 mL
Bay leaf	1	1
Prepared mustard	1 tsp.	5 mL
Ground allspice	1/4 tsp.	1 mL
Ground cloves	1/4 tsp.	1 mL
Garlic powder	1/4 tsp.	1 mL
Pepper	1/4 tsp.	1 mL
Ground cinnamon	1/4 tsp.	1 mL
Tomato juice	1 cup	250 mL
Chopped onion	2 cups	500 mL
Chopped green pepper	1/2 cup	125 mL

Measure first 12 ingredients into large saucepan.

Put second amount of tomato juice, onion and green pepper into blender. Process until smooth. Add to tomato sauce mixture. Stir. Bring to a boil. Reduce heat. Simmer, uncovered, for about 1 hour until reduced and thickened. Remove and discard bay leaf. Freeze in 1/2 cup (125 mL) portions in airtight containers or store in refrigerator for up to 2 months. Makes 5 1/2 cups (1.4 L).

2 tbsp. (30 mL): 14 Calories; trace Total Fat (0 g Mono, 0 g Poly, 0 g Sat); 0 mg Cholesterol; 3 g Carbohydrate; trace Fibre; 1 g Protein; 72 mg Sodium

Used as an ingredient in the following recipes:

Beef And Lentil Chili, page 76

Oriental Lentil Packets, page 110

Sweet And Sour Baster, page 132

Tomato Lime Marinade, page 134

Choose flavour-packed cooking oils that are low in saturated fat, such as extra-virgin olive oil, toasted sesame oil or chili-flavoured oil. Use teaspoons instead of tablespoons when measuring cooking oil, butter or margarine.

Pesto

A delicious sauce on its own, pesto is excellent when tossed with pasta, spread on a pizza base or used as a marinade for meat and vegetables. Used as an ingredient in Pesto And Tomato Pizza, page 114.

Fresh sweet basil (not dried)	2 cups	500 mL
Chickpeas, page 15	1/4 cup	60 mL
Coarsely chopped fresh parsley (not flakes)	1/4 cup	60 mL
Finely grated fresh Parmesan cheese	3 tbsp.	50 mL
Lemon juice (fresh is best)	1 tbsp.	15 mL
Granulated sugar	1/2 tsp.	2 mL
Pepper	1/4 tsp.	1 mL
Garlic clove (or 1/4 tsp., 1 mL, powder)	1	1
Vegetable Stock, page 14 (or Chicken Stock, page 12)	1/3 cup	75 mL

Process first 8 ingredients in food processor until finely chopped.

Add stock. Process until well combined. Store in refrigerator for up to 2 weeks. Makes about 3/4 cup (175 mL).

1 tbsp. (15 mL): 18 Calories; 0.7 g Total Fat (0.2 g Mono, 0.1 g Poly, 0.4 g Sat); 1 mg Cholesterol; 2 g Carbohydrate; 1 g Fibre; 1 g Protein; 36 mg Sodium

Sweet And Sour Baster

A succulent sweet and sour sauce that gives meat exquisite flavour.

Finely chopped onion	1/3 cup	75 mL
Garlic cloves, minced (or 1 tsp., 5 mL, powder)	4	4
Small fresh chili pepper (seeds removed for less heat), minced (see Note), or 1/8 tsp. (0.5 mL) cayenne pepper	1	1
Canola oil	2 tsp.	10 mL
Apple cider vinegar	1/3 cup	75 mL
Liquid honey	3 tbsp.	50 mL
Good-For-All Ketchup, page 131	1 cup	250 mL

(continued on next page)

Sauté onion, garlic and chili pepper in canola oil in large non-stick frying pan for 5 to 7 minutes until soft.

Add vinegar, honey and ketchup. Reduce heat. Simmer, uncovered, for 7 to 8 minutes, stirring occasionally, until reduced and slightly thickened. Makes 1 1/3 cups (325 mL).

2 tbsp. (30 mL): 43 Calories; 0.9 g Total Fat (0.5 g Mono, 0.3 g Poly, 0.1 g Sat); 0 mg Cholesterol; 9 g Carbohydrate; trace Fibre; 1 g Protein; 56 mg Sodium

Note: Wear gloves when chopping chili peppers and avoid touching your eyes.

Banana And Pineapple Chutney

This is perfect with barbecued steaks, chicken, lamb and pork. Cook it at the same time as your favourite marinated meat. Good with fish too.

Medium bananas, halved lengthwise and cut into 1 inch (2.5 cm) pieces	2	2
Chopped fresh pineapple (about 1/2 inch, 12 mm, pieces)	1 cup	250 mL
Brown sugar, packed	1/4 cup	60 mL
Dark rum	1/4 cup	60 mL
Malt vinegar	2 tbsp.	30 mL
Finely chopped fresh (or sliced pickled) jalapeño pepper	2 tsp.	10 mL
Salt	1/2 tsp.	2 mL
Ground cardamom	1/8 tsp.	0.5 mL

Combine all 8 ingredients in large saucepan. Cook on medium-high for 10 to 15 minutes, stirring occasionally, until banana is soft and mixture is thickened. Makes about 1 1/2 cups (375 mL).

2 tbsp. (30 mL): 41 Calories; 0.2 g Total Fat (trace Mono, trace Poly, trace Sat); 0 mg Cholesterol; 10 g Carbohydrate; 1 g Fibre; trace Protein; 78 mg Sodium

Tomato Lime Marinade

Especially delicious on grilled pork and chicken. Tangy lime and slight heat from chilies make this a delicious all 'round summer marinade. Makes enough to marinate up to 3 lbs. (1.4 kg) meat.

Good-For-All Ketchup, page 131	**1 cup**	**250 mL**
Lime juice	**1/3 cup**	**75 mL**
Tequila (optional)	**1/4 cup**	**60 mL**
Green onions, each cut into 4 pieces	**3**	**3**
Garlic cloves, halved (or 3/4 tsp., 4 mL, powder)	**3**	**3**
Dried crushed chilies	**1/2 tsp.**	**2 mL**

Process all 6 ingredients in blender until smooth. Makes about 2 cups (500 mL).

2 tbsp. (30 mL): 11 Calories; trace Total Fat (0 g Mono, trace Poly, 0 g Sat); 0 mg Cholesterol; 2 g Carbohydrate; trace Fibre; trace Protein; 36 mg Sodium

Red Pepper Sauce

This attractive and versatile sauce has a sweet, rich flavour. Serve with Fish Fingers, page 98, or Vegetable Patties, page 109.

Medium red peppers (about 3 lbs., 1.4 kg)	**6**	**6**
Garlic clove, chopped (or 1/4 tsp., 1 mL, powder)	**1**	**1**
Balsamic vinegar	**1 tbsp.**	**15 mL**
Pepper	**1/2 tsp.**	**2 mL**

Arrange whole peppers on greased baking sheet. Roast in 400°F (205°C) oven for about 45 minutes, turning occasionally, until skins are blistered and blackened. Place in large bowl. Cover. Let stand for 10 minutes until cool enough to handle. Peel and discard skin. Remove and discard seeds.

Put peppers and remaining 3 ingredients into food processor. Process until smooth. Freeze in 1/2 cup (125 mL) portions in airtight containers or resealable freezer bags. Makes 3 1/2 cups (875 mL).

2 tbsp. (30 mL): 7 Calories; trace Total Fat (0 g Mono, trace Poly, 0 g Sat); 0 mg Cholesterol; 2 g Carbohydrate; trace Fibre; trace Protein; 1 mg Sodium

Used as an ingredient in the following recipes:

Beef And Eggplant Burgers, page 78   Pesto And Tomato Pizza, page 114
Veal And Asparagus Rolls, page 80

Roasted Tomato Sauce

You'll find many creative ways to enjoy this thick tomato sauce. Use on pizzas, pastas, vegetables or crusty bread. Add a dash of chili sauce to give this a spicy kick. Serve with Vegetable Patties, page 109.

Ripe medium roma (plum) tomatoes, halved lengthwise	**20**	**20**
Granulated sugar	**2 tsp.**	**10 mL**
Pepper, sprinkle		
Water	**2 tbsp.**	**30 mL**
Chopped onion	**3/4 cup**	**175 mL**
Garlic cloves, chopped (or 1/2 tsp., 2 mL, powder)	**2**	**2**
Brown sugar, packed	**1 tbsp.**	**15 mL**
Balsamic vinegar	**2 tsp.**	**10 mL**
Indonesian sweet (or thick) soy sauce	**1 tsp.**	**5 mL**
Pepper	**1/2 tsp.**	**2 mL**

Place tomato halves, cut side up, on lightly greased baking sheets. Sprinkle with granulated sugar and first amount of pepper. Bake in 350°F (175°C) oven for about 30 minutes until tomato is soft.

Heat water in large frying pan on medium-high. Add onion and garlic. Cook for about 5 minutes, stirring occasionally, until onion is soft.

Put tomato, onion mixture and remaining 4 ingredients into food processor. Process, in 2 batches, until smooth. Freeze in 1/2 cup (125 mL) portions in airtight containers or resealable freezer bags. Makes about 5 1/2 cups (1.4 L).

1/2 cup (125 mL): 38 Calories; 0.4 g Total Fat (0.1 g Mono, 0.2 g Poly, 0.1 g Sat); 0 mg Cholesterol; 9 g Carbohydrate; 1 g Fibre; 1 g Protein; 36 mg Sodium

Used as an ingredient in the following recipes:

Full O'Beans Soup, page 68
Chicken Tomato Soup, page 69
Beef And Lentil Chili, page 76
Chicken Meatballs, page 83
Shrimp And Red Pepper Pizza, page 92

Tomato Chili Mussels, page 95
Red Scallop Vermicelli, page 97
Grilled Vegetable Kabobs, page 112
Calabacitas, page 130

Cognac Peach Dessert

A moist, melt-in-your-mouth white cake served with peaches in a sweet cognac sauce. A true delight! Cake will be fairly flat when baked.

WHITE CAKE		
Milk	1 cup	250 mL
Vanilla	1/2 tsp.	2 mL
Egg whites (large), room temperature	2	2
Cake flour (sift before measuring)	1 cup	250 mL
Granulated sugar	1 cup	250 mL
Baking powder	1 tbsp.	15 mL
COGNAC PEACH SAUCE		
Frozen peach slices	16	16
Brown sugar, packed	2/3 cup	150 mL
Ground cinnamon	1/8 tsp.	0.5 mL
Water	1/2 cup	125 mL
Cognac	1/4 cup	60 mL

White Cake: Heat milk and vanilla in small saucepan on medium, stirring occasionally, until boiling. Remove from heat.

Beat egg whites in small bowl until stiff peaks form. Set aside.

Stir flour, granulated sugar and baking powder in medium bowl. Using same beaters, slowly beat in hot milk mixture until smooth. Beat for 1 minute. Fold egg whites into batter until well combined. Turn into greased and floured 10 inch (25 cm) angel food tube pan. Bake in 300°F (150°C) oven for about 40 minutes until wooden pick inserted between edge and centre of cake comes out clean. Do not invert. Let stand in pan on wire rack for 15 minutes. Cut around side of cake to loosen. Remove from pan. Place on wire rack to cool completely. Cuts into 8 wedges.

Cognac Peach Sauce: Combine peach slices, brown sugar, cinnamon and water in large saucepan. Cover. Heat on medium-low for about 10 minutes, stirring occasionally, until peaches have thawed. Increase heat to medium-high. Boil, uncovered, for 2 minutes.

(continued on next page)

Add cognac. Heat and stir for 1 minute. Remove from heat. Let stand for about 10 minutes until cool. Remove peaches with slotted spoon, reserving syrup. Arrange 2 peach slices on each cake wedge. Drizzle reserved syrup over peaches and wedges. Serves 8.

1 serving: 332 Calories; 0.5 g Total Fat (0.1 g Mono, 0.1 g Poly, 0.2 g Sat); 1 mg Cholesterol; 80 g Carbohydrate; 4 g Fibre; 5 g Protein; 223 mg Sodium

Pictured on page 90.

Variation: Drizzle about 1/2 of reserved syrup over cake while still in pan. Let stand in pan until cool before removing and slicing. Cut cake into wedges. Arrange peaches on top. Drizzle with remaining reserved syrup. Serve with dollops of low-calorie whipped topping.

Poached Maple Pears

Pears poached in maple syrup and port with a hint of cinnamon and cloves. Serve with low-fat ice cream or custard. The perfect treat on a cold day.

Firm medium pears, peeled	4	4
Port	1 cup	250 mL
Prepared orange juice	1/2 cup	125 mL
Maple (or maple-flavoured) syrup	1/3 cup	75 mL
Cinnamon stick (4 inch, 10 cm, length)	1	1
Whole cloves	6	6
Fresh mint leaves, for garnish		

Remove cores from pears using apple corer and keeping pears whole.

Combine next 5 ingredients in medium saucepan. Add pears. Bring to a boil. Reduce heat to medium-low. Simmer, uncovered, for 15 to 20 minutes, turning occasionally, until pears are soft. Remove pears with slotted spoon. Keep warm. Remove and discard cinnamon stick and cloves. Bring port mixture to a boil. Boil, uncovered, for 10 to 15 minutes until reduced to 3/4 cup (175 mL). Lay pears on cutting board. Slice horizontally from large end, leaving 1/2 inch (12 mm) at small end intact. Place on individual serving plates. Fan out slightly. Drizzle with port mixture.

Garnish with mint. Serves 4.

1 serving: 210 Calories; 1.1 g Total Fat (trace Mono, trace Poly, trace Sat); 0 mg Cholesterol; 53 g Carbohydrate; 4 g Fibre; 1 g Protein; 8 mg Sodium

Pictured on page 143.

Dressed-Up Fruit Cups

Refreshing fruit with a tangy sauce and crunchy nuts. Good for breakfast as well as dessert or a snack.

CINNAMON WALNUTS		
Coarsely chopped walnuts	1/2 cup	125 mL
Brown sugar, packed	1 tbsp.	15 mL
Ground cinnamon	1/4 tsp.	1 mL
Medium navel oranges, peeled, quartered lengthwise and sliced	3	3
Medium cooking apple (such as McIntosh), with peel, finely diced	1	1
Firm bananas, quartered lengthwise and cut into thick slices	2	2
Kiwifruit, peeled, quartered lengthwise and sliced	2	2
Seedless red grapes, halved	1 cup	250 mL
HONEY YOGURT SAUCE		
Non-fat vanilla (or plain) yogurt	1 cup	250 mL
Liquid honey	1/4 cup	60 mL
Vanilla (optional)	1/4 tsp.	1 mL
Finely grated lemon (or orange) zest (optional)	1/4 tsp.	1 mL

Cinnamon Walnuts: Wash walnuts in hot water. Drain. Blot with paper towel to remove excess moisture. Walnuts should still be damp.

Combine brown sugar and cinnamon in small bowl. Add walnuts. Toss until walnuts are coated. Spread out on foil-lined baking sheet or aluminum pie plate. Bake in 400°F (205°C) oven for about 10 minutes until browned and toasted. Cool.

Combine next 5 ingredients in large bowl. Divide and spoon into 6 individual dessert bowls.

Honey Yogurt Sauce: Whisk all 4 ingredients in small bowl. Makes 1 cup (250 mL) sauce. Drizzle over fruit. Sprinkle walnut mixture over top. Makes 6 fruit cups.

1 fruit cup: 277 Calories; 8.1 g Total Fat (1.1 g Mono, 5.1 g Poly, 1.1 g Sat); 2 mg Cholesterol; 51 g Carbohydrate; 5 g Fibre; 5 g Protein; 32 mg Sodium

Pictured on page 36.

Kiwifruit Sorbet

Great green colour. The unique flavour of kiwifruit will be a hit when you serve this wonderful, almost creamy-textured sorbet.

Granulated sugar	**2/3 cup**	**150 mL**
Water	**2/3 cup**	**150 mL**
Ripe kiwifruit, peeled, coarsely chopped (about 1 1/2 lbs., 680 g)	**8**	**8**
Lemon juice	**2 tbsp.**	**30 mL**
Ripe kiwifruit, peeled, cut in half lengthwise and sliced, for garnish	**1**	**1**

Combine sugar and water in small saucepan. Heat and stir on low until sugar is dissolved. Increase heat to high. Bring to a boil. Do not stir. Remove from heat. Cool completely.

Put chopped kiwifruit, lemon juice and sugar syrup into food processor. Process until smooth. Pour into 9 x 9 inch (22 x 22 cm) pan lined with plastic wrap. Freeze for 2 hours. Remove from pan. Discard plastic wrap. Cut frozen mixture into pieces. Process all at once until smooth. Return to same pan lined with plastic wrap. Freeze for 4 to 6 hours until frozen. Let stand at room temperature for 5 minutes before serving.

Garnish individual servings with sliced kiwifruit. Makes about 3 1/3 cups (825 mL).

1/2 cup (125 mL): 132 Calories; 0.4 g Total Fat (trace Mono, 0.2 g Poly, trace Sat); 0 mg Cholesterol; 33 g Carbohydrate; 3 g Fibre; 1 g Protein; 5 mg Sodium

Pictured on page 126.

When purchasing kiwifruit, look for firm fruit that seem heavy for their size. Remember to avoid those that are soft or bruised. Keep firm kiwifruit in the refrigerator and let ripen on the countertop for a few days before using.

Pineapple Banana Cheesecake

A rich, creamy banana-flavoured cheesecake with a sweet pineapple topping. The coconut crust is firm, yet chewy. With only 12 grams of fat per serving, this is still much less than the traditional version! Choose a main course that is lower in fat so that you can enjoy this dessert without guilt.

CRUST

Flake coconut	3/4 cup	175 mL
All-purpose flour	1/4 cup	60 mL
Canola oil	2 tbsp.	30 mL

FILLING

Light creamed cottage cheese	2 cups	500 mL
Blocks of light cream cheese (8 oz., 250 g, each), softened, cubed	2	2
Granulated sugar	1 cup	250 mL
Cornstarch	3 tbsp.	50 mL
Ripe medium bananas, cut up	2	2
Egg whites (large)	3	3
Large egg	1	1

PINEAPPLE TOPPING

Granulated sugar	1/4 cup	60 mL
Cornstarch	1 tbsp.	15 mL
Can of crushed pineapple, with juice	14 oz.	398 mL

Crust: Combine coconut and flour in small bowl. Slowly drizzle with canola oil, while tossing with fork, until well distributed. Spray bottom of 9 inch (22 cm) springform pan with cooking spray. Press coconut mixture firmly into bottom. Bake in 350°F (175°C) oven for about 10 minutes until lightly golden. Cool. Spray sides of pan with cooking spray. Cut strips of waxed paper, 2 inches (5 cm) wide and a total of 30 inches (76 cm) long, to line side of pan. Press against side to adhere to cooking spray. This will prevent cheesecake from cracking while cooking and during cooling.

Filling: Put cottage cheese, cream cheese and sugar into food processor. Process for about 1 minute until smooth.

Add cornstarch and banana. Pulse with on/off motion several times until banana is broken up. Process for about 1 minute until smooth. Add egg whites and whole egg. Process for 5 seconds. Pour over crust. Bake in 450°F (230°C) oven for 10 minutes. Reduce heat to 250°F (120°C). Bake for about 1 1/2 hours until surface appears solid but when lightly shaken, centre jiggles slightly. Let stand in pan on wire rack until set and cooled.

(continued on next page)

Pineapple Topping: Combine sugar and cornstarch in small saucepan. Add pineapple with juice. Stir. Heat and stir on medium until boiling and slightly thickened. Cool for 15 minutes. Spread over filling. Chill until cold. Remove side of pan. Remove and discard waxed paper. Cuts into 12 wedges.

1 wedge: 321 Calories; 12 g Total Fat (1.7 g Mono, 0.8 g Poly, 7.1 g Sat); 39 mg Cholesterol; 41 g Carbohydrate; 1 g Fibre; 11 g Protein; 400 mg Sodium

Pictured on page 143.

Bowl Method Variation: Beat cottage cheese, cream cheese and sugar in large bowl until smooth. Mash banana with fork in small bowl. Add to cottage cheese mixture. Add cornstarch, egg whites and egg. Beat until smooth. Proceed as above.

Rhubarb Crumble

You'll wonder why you didn't put rhubarb and pineapple together sooner! The tartness of the fruit is mellowed by the oat and brown sugar topping. Serve with low-fat vanilla ice cream.

Frozen sliced rhubarb, thawed	2 1/2 cups	625 mL
Can of pineapple tidbits, well drained	14 oz.	398 mL
Brown sugar, packed	1/3 cup	75 mL
Ground nutmeg	1/2 tsp.	2 mL
Rolled oats (not instant)	3/4 cup	175 mL
Brown sugar, packed	2/3 cup	150 mL
Applesauce	1/4 cup	60 mL

Combine first 4 ingredients in medium bowl. Spoon into greased 8 x 8 inch (20 x 20 cm) pan.

Combine rolled oats, second amount of brown sugar and applesauce in separate medium bowl. Sprinkle over rhubarb mixture. Bake, uncovered, in 350°F (175°C) oven for about 30 minutes until browned. Serves 6.

1 serving: 209 Calories; 0.8 g Total Fat (0.2 g Mono, 0.3 g Poly, 0.2 g Sat); 0 mg Cholesterol; 50 g Carbohydrate; 3 g Fibre; 2 g Protein; 16 mg Sodium

Pictured on page 125.

Mango Strawberry Jelly

A refreshingly cool and creamy dessert to finish off the meal.

Envelopes of unflavoured gelatin (1/4 oz., 7 g, each)	2	2
Mango juice (found in Asian section of grocery store) or water	1/2 cup	125 mL
Granulated sugar	1/4 cup	60 mL
Can of sliced mango with syrup	14 oz.	398 mL
Non-fat vanilla yogurt	1/2 cup	125 mL
Sliced fresh strawberries	3/4 cup	175 mL

Sprinkle gelatin over mango juice in small saucepan. Let stand for 5 minutes. Add sugar. Heat and stir on medium until gelatin and sugar are dissolved.

Put mango with syrup into blender. Process until completely smooth. Pour into medium bowl.

Add gelatin mixture and yogurt. Whisk until combined. Chill for about 40 minutes, stirring occasionally, until starting to thicken.

Fold in strawberries. Pour strawberry mixture into lightly greased 4 cup (1 L) mold. Chill for at least 2 hours or overnight until firm. Loosen jelly in mold. Invert onto dampened serving plate. (Dampness makes it easier to centre mold on plate.) Serves 8.

1 serving: 99 Calories; 0.5 g Total Fat (0.2 g Mono, 0.1 g Poly, 0.2 g Sat); 1 mg Cholesterol; 23 g Carbohydrate; 1 g Fibre; 3 g Protein; 16 mg Sodium

Pictured on page 144.

1. Pineapple Banana Cheesecake, page 140
2. Poached Maple Pears, page 137

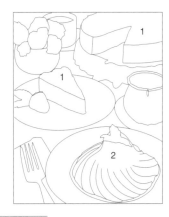

Frozen Chocolate Yogurt

This creamy, frozen treat will delight your mouth with its rich chocolate flavour.

Skim evaporated milk	3/4 cup	175 mL
Cocoa, sifted if lumpy	1/4 cup	60 mL
Granulated sugar	1/2 cup	125 mL
Low-fat plain (or vanilla) yogurt	2 cups	500 mL
Cold egg whites (large), fork-beaten	2	2
Vanilla	1 1/2 tsp.	7 mL

Heat evaporated milk in small saucepan, stirring occasionally, until boiling.

Mix cocoa and sugar in medium bowl. Add boiling evaporated milk. Stir. Chill for several hours or overnight.

Stir in yogurt, egg whites and vanilla. Pour into 1 quart (1 L) ice-cream maker. Freeze according to manufacturer's directions. Allow to soften in refrigerator for about 30 minutes before serving. Makes about 3 1/3 cups (825 mL).

1/2 cup (125 mL): 157 Calories; 1.4 g Total Fat (0.4 g Mono, trace Poly, 0.9 g Sat); 5 mg Cholesterol; 30 g Carbohydrate; 1 g Fibre; 7 g Protein; 96 mg Sodium

Pictured on page 144.

CHOCOLATE MOCHA YOGURT: Add 1 1/2 tsp. (7 mL) instant coffee granules, crushed to fine powder, and 1/8 tsp. (0.5 mL) ground cinnamon to boiling evaporated milk. Heat and stir until coffee is dissolved. Proceed with method as above.

1. Mango Strawberry Jelly, page 142
2. Frozen Chocolate Yogurt, above
3. Grilled Spiced Pineapple, page 148

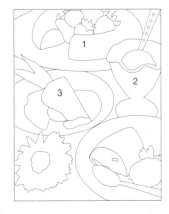

Angelic Berry Dessert

A light angel food dessert with a juicy, berry filling. This freezes well either cut or uncut. The perfect dessert when "company's coming!"

FILLING

Frozen mixed berries (or two 21 oz., 600 g, bags)	**8 cups**	**2 L**
Purple grape juice	**1 cup**	**250 mL**
Granulated sugar	**1/3 cup**	**75 mL**
Cornstarch	**1 tbsp.**	**15 mL**
Orange-flavoured liqueur (such as Grand Marnier) or grape juice	**1/4 cup**	**60 mL**
Angel food cake mix, prepared according to package directions (see Note)	**1**	**1**

Filling: Thaw berries in strainer over large bowl, reserving juice. Measure 3/4 cup (175 mL) reserved juice into medium saucepan. Add grape juice.

Mix sugar and cornstarch in small dish. Add to grape juice mixture. Heat and stir on medium-high until boiling and slightly thickened. Remove from heat. Cool for 20 minutes.

Fold in berries and liqueur.

Brush or rub brown bits from cake, making as white as possible. 1) Cut cake horizontally into 4 layers. 2) Cut layers **A** and **B** into quarters. Cut one quarter in half. 3) Line 3 quart (3 L) round casserole or mixing bowl with plastic wrap. Fit layer **C** in bottom. Stuff centre hole with 1 **bb** piece. Reserve remaining **bb** piece. 4) Line side of casserole with remaining 7 **a** and **b** quarter pieces, alternating wide and narrow ends to fit. Fill centre hollow with berry mixture. Lay remaining layer **D** over top. Stuff centre hole with reserved **bb** piece to completely enclose berry mixture. Cover with plastic wrap directly on cake surface. Press down slightly with hand to fill any air spaces and make even. Place flat plate on top of plastic wrap. Weight with 2 unopened 14 oz. (398 mL) cans. Chill for at least 8 hours or overnight. Remove and discard plastic wrap. Invert dessert onto serving plate. Remove and discard remaining plastic wrap. Cuts into 12 wedges.

(continued on next page)

1 wedge: 240 Calories; 0.3 g Total Fat (trace Mono, 0.2 g Poly, trace Sat); 0 mg Cholesterol; 57 g Carbohydrate; 4 g Fibre; 5 g Protein; 372 mg Sodium

Pictured on page 126.

Note: A 1 lb. (454 g) angel food cake is needed and generally, pre-made angel food cakes purchased in the grocery store are too small because they only weigh 10 to 12 oz. (285 to 340 g).

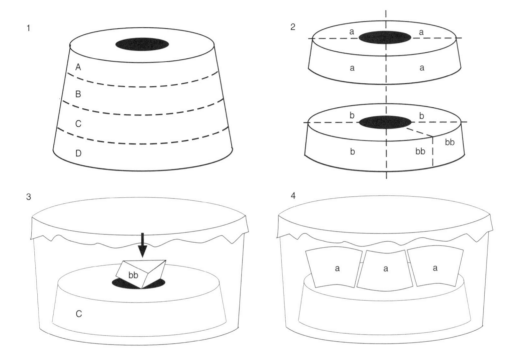

Grilled Spiced Pineapple

Ripe, juicy pineapple slices are absolutely delicious when flavoured with maple syrup and brandy and topped with this ricotta sauce. A simple, yet elegant dessert that can be served warm or cold.

Maple (or maple-flavoured) syrup	1/2 cup	125 mL
Brandy	2 tbsp.	30 mL
Ground cinnamon	1/2 tsp.	2 mL
Ground ginger	1/2 tsp.	2 mL
Pepper	1/4 tsp.	1 mL
Fresh whole pineapple, peeled, cut into 1/2 inch (12 mm) thick slices	1	1
RICOTTA SAUCE		
Ricotta cheese	1 cup	250 mL
Low-fat vanilla yogurt	1/2 cup	125 mL

Combine first 5 ingredients in small bowl. Reserve 2 tbsp. (30 mL).

Brush remaining maple syrup mixture over both sides of each pineapple slice. Cook on greased electric grill over medium heat for 3 to 5 minutes per side until browned. Cut each slice in half.

Ricotta Sauce: Combine ricotta cheese, yogurt and reserved maple syrup mixture in medium bowl. Makes about 1 1/2 cups (375 mL) sauce. Serve with pineapple. Serves 6.

1 serving: 259 Calories; 6.7 g Total Fat (1.8 g Mono, 0.5 g Poly, 3.8 g Sat); 23 mg Cholesterol; 46 g Carbohydrate; 2 g Fibre; 7 g Protein; 55 mg Sodium

Pictured on page 144.

Variation: Omit fresh pineapple slices. Use about ten canned pineapple slices, drained. Cook on greased electric grill for 1 to 2 minutes until browned.

To increase the intake of soy (a high-quality plant protein source) in your diet, use soy milk in smoothies, have a soy burger instead of a hamburger or add cubed tofu to stir-fries.

Crisp Meringue Cream Pies

A sweet banana custard in crisp, white meringue cups. The gingersnap crumbs add a subtle spicy flavour. A fun and attractive dessert.

Egg whites (large), room temperature	**6**	**6**
Granulated sugar	**1 1/2 cups**	**375 mL**
Granulated sugar	**1/2 cup**	**125 mL**
Custard powder	**1/4 cup**	**60 mL**
All-purpose flour	**2 tbsp.**	**30 mL**
Can of skim evaporated milk	**13 1/2 oz.**	**385 mL**
Milk	**3/4 cup**	**175 mL**
Vanilla (or banana flavouring)	**1 tsp.**	**5 mL**
Diced banana	**1 1/2 cups**	**375 mL**
Gingersnaps, crushed into crumbs	**2**	**2**

Beat egg whites in large bowl until soft peaks form. Add first amount of sugar, 2 tbsp. (30 mL) at a time, until stiff peaks form and sugar is dissolved. Draw or mark eight 3 to 3 1/2 inch (7.5 to 9 cm) circles on parchment paper or foil. Turn paper over onto baking sheet. Fill circles with meringue, spreading or piping into even layer. Pipe remaining meringue around edges in dollops to build up sides to about 2 inches (5 cm) high. Bake on centre rack in 200°F (95°C) oven for 2 to 3 hours until dry. Turn oven off. Let meringues stand in oven until cool.

Stir second amount of sugar, custard powder and flour in medium saucepan. Slowly stir in evaporated milk and milk until smooth. Cook on medium, stirring often, until boiling and thickened. Reduce heat to medium-low. Cook for 1 minute. Remove from heat.

Stir in vanilla and banana. Cover with plastic wrap directly on surface to prevent skin from forming. Cool. Spoon scant 1/2 cup (125 mL) milk mixture into meringues just before or up to 1 hour before serving.

Sprinkle with gingersnap crumbs. Makes 8 pies.

1 pie: 324 Calories; 0.6 g Total Fat (0.2 g Mono, 0.1 g Poly, 0.3 g Sat); 1 mg Cholesterol; 74 g Carbohydrate; 1 g Fibre; 7 g Protein; 130 mg Sodium

Pictured on page 126 and on back cover.

Saucy Hot Fruit Packets

This delectable dessert is crispy and pastry-like on the outside with soft, sweet fruit on the inside. Each packet is large enough to satisfy any craving, but can be shared easily.

ORANGE SAUCE

Cornstarch	1 tbsp.	15 mL
Granulated sugar	1 tbsp.	15 mL
Prepared orange juice	2/3 cup	150 mL
Finely grated orange zest	1/2 tsp.	2 mL
Orange-flavoured liqueur (such as Grand Marnier)	2 tbsp.	30 mL
Medium bananas, cut into 1/4 inch (6 mm) slices	2	2
Fresh (or frozen, thawed) blueberries	2/3 cup	150 mL
Large whole wheat flour tortillas (about 10 inches, 25 cm)	4	4
Miniature marshmallows	2/3 cup	150 mL
Non-fat vanilla (or blueberry) yogurt	3/4 cup	175 mL
Ground cinnamon, sprinkle		

Orange Sauce: Stir cornstarch and sugar in small saucepan. Add orange juice and zest. Heat and stir on medium until boiling and slightly thickened.

Stir in liqueur. Makes 3/4 cup (175 mL) sauce. Set aside.

Divide and arrange banana slices and blueberries down centre of tortillas.

Combine marshmallows and yogurt in small bowl. Divide and spoon over fruit. Roll up tortillas, tucking in sides, to enclose filling. Arrange, seam-side down, on greased baking sheet.

Spray tortillas with cooking spray. Sprinkle lightly with cinnamon. Bake in 425°F (220°C) oven for about 10 minutes until lightly golden and crisp. Drizzle about 2 1/2 tbsp. (37 mL) sauce over each packet. Makes 4 packets.

1 packet with sauce: 351 Calories; 5.1 g Total Fat (2.2 g Mono, 0.9 g Poly, 1.3 g Sat); 2 mg Cholesterol; 70 g Carbohydrate; 2 g Fibre; 8 g Protein; 316 mg Sodium

Measurement Tables

Throughout this book measurements are given in Conventional and Metric measure. To compensate for differences between the two measurements due to rounding, a full metric measure is not always used. The cup used is the standard 8 fluid ounce. Temperature is given in degrees Fahrenheit and Celsius. Baking pan measurements are in inches and centimetres as well as quarts and litres. An exact metric conversion is given below as well as the working equivalent (Standard Measure).

OVEN TEMPERATURES

Fahrenheit (°F)	Celsius (°C)
175°	80°
200°	95°
225°	110°
250°	120°
275°	140°
300°	150°
325°	160°
350°	175°
375°	190°
400°	205°
425°	220°
450°	230°
475°	240°
500°	260°

SPOONS

Conventional Measure	Metric Exact Conversion Millilitre (mL)	Metric Standard Measure Millilitre (mL)
$1/8$ teaspoon (tsp.)	0.6 mL	0.5 mL
$1/4$ teaspoon (tsp.)	1.2 mL	1 mL
$1/2$ teaspoon (tsp.)	2.4 mL	2 mL
1 teaspoon (tsp.)	4.7 mL	5 mL
2 teaspoons (tsp.)	9.4 mL	10 mL
1 tablespoon (tbsp.)	14.2 mL	15 mL

CUPS

	Metric Exact Conversion	Metric Standard Measure
$1/4$ cup (4 tbsp.)	56.8 mL	60 mL
$1/3$ cup ($5^1/3$ tbsp.)	75.6 mL	75 mL
$1/2$ cup (8 tbsp.)	113.7 mL	125 mL
$2/3$ cup ($10^2/3$ tbsp.)	151.2 mL	150 mL
$3/4$ cup (12 tbsp.)	170.5 mL	175 mL
1 cup (16 tbsp.)	227.3 mL	250 mL
$4^1/2$ cups	1022.9 mL	1000 mL (1 L)

PANS

Conventional Inches	Metric Centimetres
8x8 inch	20x20 cm
9x9 inch	22x22 cm
9x13 inch	22x33 cm
10x15 inch	25x38 cm
11x17 inch	28x43 cm
8x2 inch round	20x5 cm
9x2 inch round	22x5 cm
$10x4^1/2$ inch tube	25x11 cm
8x4x3 inch loaf	20x10x7.5 cm
9x5x3 inch loaf	22x12.5x7.5 cm

DRY MEASUREMENTS

Conventional Measure Ounces (oz.)	Metric Exact Conversion Grams (g)	Metric Standard Measure Grams (g)
1 oz.	28.3 g	28 g
2 oz.	56.7 g	57 g
3 oz.	85.0 g	85 g
4 oz.	113.4 g	125 g
5 oz.	141.7 g	140 g
6 oz.	170.1 g	170 g
7 oz.	198.4 g	200 g
8 oz.	226.8 g	250 g
16 oz.	453.6 g	500 g
32 oz.	907.2 g	1000 g (1 kg)

CASSEROLES (Canada & Britain)

Standard Size Casserole	Exact Metric Measure
1 qt. (5 cups)	1.13 L
$1^1/2$ qts. ($7^1/2$ cups)	1.69 L
2 qts. (10 cups)	2.25 L
$2^1/2$ qts. ($12^1/2$ cups)	2.81 L
3 qts. (15 cups)	3.38 L
4 qts. (20 cups)	4.5 L
5 qts. (25 cups)	5.63 L

CASSEROLES (United States)

Standard Size Casserole	Exact Metric Measure
1 qt. (4 cups)	900 mL
$1^1/2$ qts. (6 cups)	1.35 L
2 qts. (8 cups)	1.8 L
$2^1/2$ qts. (10 cups)	2.25 L
3 qts. (12 cups)	2.7 L
4 qts. (16 cups)	3.6 L
5 qts. (20 cups)	4.5 L

Tip Index

Recipe Index

Company's Coming cookbooks are available at **retail locations** throughout Canada!

See mail order form

Buy any 2 cookbooks—choose a 3rd FREE of equal or less value than the lowest price paid.   *Available in French

Original Series   CA$14.99 Canada   US$10.99 USA & International

CODE		CODE		CODE	
SQ	150 Delicious Squares*	CH	Chicken, Etc.*	SCH	Stews, Chilies & Chowders
CA	Casseroles*	KC	Kids Cooking	FD	Fondues
MU	Muffins & More*	CT	Cooking For Two*	CCBE	The Beef Book
SA	Salads*	BB	Breakfasts & Brunches*	ASI	Asian Cooking
AP	Appetizers	SC	Slow Cooker Recipes*	CB	The Cheese Book
DE	Desserts	ODM	One Dish Meals*	RC	The Rookie Cook
SS	Soups & Sandwiches	ST	Starters*	RHR	Rush-Hour Recipes
CO	Cookies*	SF	Stir-Fry*	SW	Sweet Cravings
PA	Pasta*	MAM	Make-Ahead Meals*	YRG	Year-Round Grilling **NEW**
BA	Barbecues*	PB	The Potato Book*		*March 1, 2003*
LR	Light Recipes*	CCLFC	Low-Fat Cooking*		
PR	Preserves*	CCLFP	Low-Fat Pasta*		
		CFK	Cook For Kids		

Greatest Hits Series

CODE	CA$12.99 Canada US$9.99 USA & International
ITAL	Italian
MEX	Mexican

Lifestyle Series

CODE	CA$16.99 Canada US$12.99 USA & International
GR	Grilling
DC	Diabetic Cooking

CODE	CA$19.99 Canada US$17.99 USA & International
HC	Heart-Friendly Cooking

Special Occasion Series

CODE	CA$19.99 Canada US$17.99 USA & International
CE	Chocolate Everything
GFK	Gifts from the Kitchen
CFS	Cooking for the Seasons

CODE	CA$24.99 Canada US$19.99 USA & International
HFH	Home for the Holidays

www.**companys**coming.com
visit our ↑ web-site

COMPANY'S COMING PUBLISHING LIMITED
2311 - 96 Street
Edmonton, Alberta, Canada T6N 1G3
Tel: (780) 450-6223 Fax: (780) 450-1857

Mail Order Form

See page 158 for list of cookbooks

QUANTITY	CODE	TITLE	PRICE EACH	PRICE TOTAL
			$	$

DON'T FORGET to indicate your FREE book(s). (see exclusive mail order offer above) PLEASE PRINT

	TOTAL BOOKS (including FREE)		**TOTAL BOOKS PURCHASED:**	$

		INTERNATIONAL		CANADA & USA	
Plus Shipping & Handling (PER DESTINATION)		$ 7.00	(one book)	$ 5.00	(1-3 books)
Additional Books (INCLUDING FREE BOOKS)		$	($2.00 each)	$	($1.00 each)
SUB-TOTAL		$		$	
Canadian residents add G.S.T(7%)				$	
TOTAL AMOUNT ENCLOSED		$		$	

The Fine Print

☐ MasterCard   ☐ VISA

Expiry date _____

Account # _____

Name of cardholder _____

Cardholder's signature _____

Shipping Address

Send the cookbooks listed above to:

Name: _____

Street: _____

City: _____   Prov./State: _____

Country: _____   Postal Code/Zip: _____

Tel: (___) _____

E-mail address: _____

Gift Giving

- Let us help you with your gift giving!
- We will send cookbooks directly to the recipients of your choice if you give us their names and addresses.
- Please specify the titles you wish to send to each person.
- If you would like to include your personal note or card, we will be pleased to enclose it with your gift order.
- Company's Coming Cookbooks make excellent gifts: Birthdays, bridal showers, Mother's Day, Father's Day, graduation or any occasion... collect them all!

Canada's most
popular
cookbooks